KINGFISHER

First published 2013 by Kingfisher
an imprint of Macmillan Children's Books
a division of Macmillan Publishers Limited
20 New Wharf Road, London N1 9RR
Basingstoke and Oxford
Associated companies throughout the world
www.panmacmillan.com

Edited by: Andrea Mills

Designed by: Samantha Richiardi

Developed by: Jo Connor and Simon Holland

Art director: Mike Davis

ISBN 978-0-7534-3622-6

Copyright © Macmillan Children's Books 2013

2 4 6 8 9 7 5 3 1

1TR/0213/WKT/UG/128MA

A CIP catalogue record for this book is available
from the British Library.

Printed in China

THINK AGAIN!

CLIVE GIFFORD

KINGFISHER

EVERYTHING YOU KNOW IS WRONG*

IT'S SCANDALOUS. HOW DID THIS HAPPEN?

Well, the truth can be distorted in different ways. Some writers get it wrong from the start or they present their opinions as pure fact. Others copy this information without questioning it or shorten and summarize facts from reliable sources, but miss out vital points as a result. A lot of myths and mistakes are spread by word of mouth or via emails, blogs and websites, as many people love gossip and rumour. Over time, the most repeated myths become accepted as facts.

Knowledge is evolving continually. Discoveries about how things work or how things were in the past are being made all the time. The idea of new innovations may seem unlikely or pure science fiction. But amazing developments in technology – such as the Internet, personal communications, space travel and replacement body parts – have quickly become scientific fact.

This bumper book is packed with the misconceptions, myths, errors, falsehoods and bonkers theories that have somehow gained status as facts. It explains what the real facts are and, in some cases, how the wrong facts caught on. So if you think everything you know is 100 per cent correct... THINK AGAIN.

The truth is out there – only it is sometimes very different to what you thought it was.

*OKAY, NOT QUITE EVERYTHING, BUT A SURPRISINGLY LARGE AMOUNT.

CHALLENGE THE LIES

The following statements, which you will find in each chapter of this book, are WRONG. This book will tell you WHY they are wrong and show you what is RIGHT.

CHAPTER 1: BODY BLOOPERS

CHAPTER 2: ANIMAL ERRORS

CHAPTER 3: SCIENCE SLIP-UPS

CHAPTER 4: HISTORIC HOWLERS

CHAPTER 5: WORLD WONDERS AND BLUNDERS

BODY BLOOPERS

CHAPTER 1

Your body is amazing. It's packed full of incredible organs and systems, from your kidneys (containing one million tiny filters that remove waste from your blood) to your brain (enabling you to do many things at once and think about 70,000 thoughts in a single day).

But as great as you are, your body isn't perfect. You cannot lick your elbow and neither do your eyes and brain always get things right. Similarly, neither is our knowledge of the human body and how it works. What we know about the human body has grown enormously in recent years. This means that some old or commonly held beliefs about our body's parts, health, diet and diseases are wrong, wrong, WRONG!

BONY BLUNDERS

ERROR 1: HUMANS ALWAYS HAVE THE SAME NUMBER OF BONES

'The human skeleton is made up of 206 bones.' You'll find this or similar sentences in a whole library full of books about the human body. But, like so many things, that statement is not quite right and here's why: the body of a typical adult human may have 206 bones, but some people have more or less bones.

As a baby you are born with more than 270 parts to your skeleton, not 206. Many of these parts harden and come together to form your adult bones as you grow up. One in around 500 children is born with at least one extra finger or toe, complete with additional bones. This is known as polydactylism. Some have these extra digits surgically removed while others keep them.

Six fingers on each hand, for example, didn't stop Antonio Alfonseca from becoming a successful Major League Baseball pitcher in the USA.

And did you know that a baby's kneecaps won't show up as bones on an X-ray? The kneecaps start out as pieces of tough tissue called cartilage, which X-rays don't detect. It takes a few years for the kneecaps to be replaced by hard bone.

ERROR 2: EVERYONE HAS 12 SETS OF RIBS

Not quite everyone, actually. Scientific researchers have discovered that sometimes a person is born with an extra pair of ribs, known as cervical ribs. Estimates vary from one in every 500 to as many as one in every 20 people. It's another reason why not everyone in the world has 206 bones in their body.

ERROR 3: EVERY ADULT HAS 32 TEETH

You know that your milk (or baby) teeth fall out and are replaced by your adult set of gnashers. These consist of an upper and lower set that each have 16 teeth, but four of these teeth can be very late arrivals. Your wisdom teeth are four molars (blocky teeth used to grind food), which usually appear only in your late teens at the very back of your mouth. In many thousands of cases they never appear at all, leaving someone with 28 teeth – still plenty to chow down with. And there's more! A handful of people around the world have hyperdontia – more than 32 adult teeth.

ERROR 4: YOU REMAIN THE SAME HEIGHT THROUGHOUT THE DAY

If you start the day 143cm tall, you'd think you'd end the day precisely the same height. Afraid not! After getting up in the morning, you actually shrink by a small amount during the day – by about 1–1.5cm on average. This is due to the force of gravity, which presses down on your spine and compresses the discs of cartilage in between each of the vertebrae (the bones that make up your spine). When you lie down to sleep at night, the cartilage eases back into shape and you become your normal height again.

HUMERUS

RIBS

COCCYX

SPLITTING HAIRS

ERROR 1 MOST OF YOUR HAIR IS ON YOUR HEAD

It might be the longest and most noticeable hair, but that stuff on your head you spend hours washing, brushing and grooming does not make up most of your hairy story.

A typical head of hair has 100,000–150,000 individual hairs. However, that amount is dwarfed by the numbers of hairs that grow over almost all your body – except certain areas such as your lips, the soles of your feet and the palms of your hands. Estimates put the number of body hairs at about five million. You don't pay much attention to these hairs because they are very fine.

ERROR 2 — SUDDEN SHOCKS TURN YOUR HAIR WHITE OVERNIGHT

Bet you've seen a film or cartoon where a sudden surprise turns a character's hair white instantly. In real life, it simply cannot happen that fast. Hair colour comes from a chemical called melanin, which enters the hair at the base of the follicle. The lighter the colour of someone's hair, the less melanin it contains. Grey and white hairs contain almost no melanin.

The part of the hair that emerges above the skin is dead. This means it cannot change its colour naturally. A change of colour would be caused by the growth of new hair containing less or no melanin, so it may take months for a head of hair to turn from black or brunette to bright white!

There is one shocking reaction that is caused by hair – and that's goosebumps. When you're startled, chilled or frightened, you may develop lots of tiny bumps on your skin for a moment or two. These are caused by your body hairs being pulled upright by tiny muscles attached to the hair follicles.

ERROR 3 — HAIR GROWS BACK THICKER AND FASTER AFTER IT IS SHAVED OR CUT

This is an old wives' tale that still persists to this day. Cutting hair may make it look healthier because the damaged ends are removed. It may also make the shortened hair look a little thicker, as hairs are slightly thicker at their base than at their tip. But cutting doesn't stimulate new, thicker growth or make your hair grow at a faster rate than before. A typical person's hair grows at about 13mm a month – just over 15cm a year.

ERROR 4 — SPLIT ENDS CAN BE REPAIRED BY CONDITIONERS

For those spending all their pocket money on luxury shampoos and conditioners, here is some bad news. The hair that you are washing above your scalp is already dead, so it cannot truly be repaired. Many conditioners contain chemicals that act as bonding agents, but these only stick the split ends of the hairs together for a short time, and are usually rinsed away the next time you wash.

MIGHTILY WRONG

 ## ERROR 1: A MUSCLE PUSHES AND PULLS YOUR BODY'S PARTS AROUND

Muscling into our myths and misconceptions comes what sounds like the perfectly sensible statement above... only it's half right and half wrong.

Of course, your muscles do move your body parts around. Without them you couldn't walk, talk, breathe, blink or produce facial expressions, but none of the 630 skeletal muscles in your body ever do any pushing. All they can ever do is pull in one direction.

Each skeletal muscle is a collection of bundles of nerve cells and fibres. These muscles are mostly joined to bones by strong tendons. When a nerve signal is sent from the brain, a muscle can contract, getting shorter and pulling the bone it is connected to towards the muscle. But what happens when you want to move that part back to its original position or in a different direction? Well, your body's muscles are grouped with muscles able to contract and pull in different directions. These ingenious arrangements are called antagonistic pairs.

ERROR 3: IF YOU DON'T EXERCISE FOR A LONG TIME, MUSCLE TURNS TO FAT

About 40 per cent of your entire body weight is muscle. Exercising regularly can build muscle, making muscle cells a little larger. However, if you don't exercise for a long time, your muscle cells can shrink a little, losing some of your body's tone. But muscle and fat are completely different types of body tissue and one cannot be turned into the other. You will simply put on weight as extra fat if you stop exercising and eat too much junk food. So, avoid being a couch potato!

ERROR 2: YOU CAN CONTROL ALL YOUR MUSCLE MOVEMENTS

Nearly all skeletal muscles are moved by voluntary thoughts from your brain. When you want to reach for the TV's remote control, for example, your brain sends signals to the muscles of your back, arm and hand to help you lean forward and grab it. Yet, skeletal muscle is just one of three types of muscle in your body. The other two work without you even having to think about them. Smooth muscle helps move foods and fluids around your internal organs, such as your stomach and small intestine. Cardiac muscle is the powerful muscle in your heart that allows it to pump blood around your body every moment of every day. If you had to think about it every time, you'd be exhausted!

HARD TO DIGEST

 JUNK FOOD CAUSES TEENAGE SPOTS

If you're a teenager, chances are you'll get spots. Most teens suffer from *acne vulgaris*, a skin condition in which whiteheads, blackheads and pus-filled pimples break out from the pores.

Eating a diet that is mostly free of junk foods, fats and sugars is good for a teenager's health, including their skin, but the links between greasy burgers and greasy skin are seriously overrated. The root cause of most acne is found in the pores of the skin, where hair follicles are fed by sebum. This oily substance is produced in the sebaceous glands. As a teenager's body develops, the hormones released can prompt it to produce too much sebum. This mixes with dead skin cells to clog up the pores of the skin, trapping bacteria inside that then multiply and inflame the pore. And that's zit, in a nutshell!

SUGAR MAKES PEOPLE HYPERACTIVE

ERROR 2

Too much sugar can cause weight gain and tooth decay. It may also be responsible for a drop in your overall blood-sugar levels and make you slightly irritable and distracted, but it doesn't make you run around the room like a mad thing! More than 12 scientific studies have failed to find a direct link between sugar and hyperactivity.

In one study, published in the *Journal of Abnormal Child Psychology*, children were given a sugar-free drink. Half of the parents were told it was high in sugar, while the other half were told it was sugar free. The mothers who reported that their children were hyperactive afterwards were those who believed the drink was packed full of sugar.

So why does this myth persist? Part of the reason may be parties. Kids get excited at these events, where there just happens to be sugary food served. However, it's the fun, games and a room full of kids that cause the energetic behaviour – not the food.

EATING TURKEY MAKES PEOPLE ESPECIALLY DROWSY

ERROR 3

Turkey meat contains an amino acid called tryptophan. Taken at the right times and in the right doses, this chemical can make people feel drowsy. But the amount of tryptophan in turkey is not high. Cheese and pork contain more. So where does this turkey of an idea originate? Many think it's because turkeys are traditionally served at Thanksgiving dinner in the USA and at Christmas dinner in some parts of the world. These tend to be large, heavy meals that use up energy as your body digests them, making you feel sleepy. Zzzzz.

MEASURED FOUR SQUARE METRES AND CONTAINED AROUND 29 MILLION CALORIES.

FOOLED BY FOOD

ERROR 1 CARROTS IMPROVE YOUR EYESIGHT

Carrots do contain quantities of vitamin A, which helps keep eyes healthy, but can carrots improve your eyesight or give you night vision like a superhero's? No way.

This false fact may have stemmed from World War II (1939–45). During this war, the British claimed that their pilots feasted on carrots before shooting down enemy aircraft. This untruthful piece of storytelling was designed to cover up the real reason for their success – a radar system that gave early warning of incoming enemy aircraft.

ERROR 2 EATING SPINACH MAKES YOU STRONG

Iron is an important mineral because it helps blood deliver oxygen round your body. A lack of iron can leave you feeling tired and weak. Eating spinach will give your body some iron, but not as much as other foods such as liver, red meat and seafood do. So, why did spinach steal the show for being richer in iron than other foods? No one is quite certain.

VEGETARIANS DO NOT GET ENOUGH PROTEIN IN THEIR DIET

ERROR 3

Vegetarians choose not to eat meat, fish and other creatures for lots of different reasons. Some simply don't like the taste or they believe going veggie can be more healthy. Others don't like animals being killed for food or they think vegetarian foods use less of the planet's resources in their production. But don't argue with a vegetarian, thinking they won't have the strength or stamina to argue back. A good vegetarian diet can contain plenty of protein, which is essential for growth and health.

Nutritionists recommend you consume about 0.8–1g of protein per kilogram you weigh every day. So, if you're a 40kg boy or girl, you'll need 32–40g of protein a day from your grub. While meat and fish are strong sources of protein, many other foods that can form part of a vegetarian diet are full of protein as well. These include nuts, sunflower and pumpkin seeds, large beans, milk, cheese and eggs. A single boiled egg contains 6g of protein, but soybeans can contain as much as 39g of protein per 100g served – that's more protein-packed than many cuts of meat.

AND REFERS TO THE VINEGAR RICE USED IN MANY SUSHI DISHES.

HEADS UP!

ERROR 1 ATTENTION ALL HUMANS! YOU USE ONLY 10 PER CENT OF YOUR BRAIN

Many books, articles on the Internet and even positive-thinking gurus say the same thing... people use only one-tenth of their brain's capacity. "Unleash your potential," they cry. "Just imagine what you could achieve if you DID use the other 90 per cent of your brain!" The only problem with this idea is that it's wrong!

Scientists know that damage to a small part of the brain can lead to a great change in a person's ability to function. This fact applies to most parts of the brain. So, that must mean that most of the brain is important and is used. Science can back this up in several ways. Medical scanners, such as MRI (magnetic resonance imaging) machines, have peered inside the brain and seen much of it active at the same time.

ERROR 2 — YOU CAN THINK SO MUCH IT HURTS

Impossible. Your brain does not have any of the nerve cells, called pain receptors, that are found in other parts of your body. This means your actual brain cannot detect if it is suffering any pain, which is why some brain surgery is performed while the patient is wide awake.

ERROR 3 — DIFFERENT PARTS OF THE BRAIN FUNCTION ONE AT A TIME

False! If you eat your dinner as you read these words, then you are using at least six different parts of your brain at once. The occipital lobes help you process what you can see in front of you, your frontal lobes let you think and reason, the parietal lobes allow you to sense and enjoy the taste, smell and texture of the food, and the temporal lobes enable you to understand sounds. Your cerebellum helps you sit, balance and hold this book, while the hippocampus assists you with remembering words. That's not taking into account all the other parts of your brain working to help you breathe and keep your body parts running. It all adds up to a lot more than 10 per cent!

MAKING SENSE OF IT

ERROR 1 HUMAN BEINGS HAVE FIVE SENSES

Human beings do have the five senses of sight, hearing, touch, smell and taste, but that's only part of the story. They also have a whole load of other senses as well, between 9 and 21 in total. These include the sense of pain from skin or joints, called nociception, and the sense of the body feeling and reporting back heat to the brain, called thermoception.

There's also your sense of balance, called equilibrioception. Tiny canals containing liquid in your inner ear act a bit like spirit levels to send signals back to your brain. They work with your eyes and a whole extra sense, called proprioception – the sense of knowing where the parts of your body are positioned – to help you balance.

If you don't believe in proprioception, close your eyes and keep them shut. Now, stretch out your arm, point a finger and slowly bring the finger back to touch your nose. Did you succeed? You should, as your sense of knowing where your body parts are should help you to locate your nose.

Though scientists may disagree on exactly how many senses there are in total, they all agree that there are more than five.

ERROR 2 YOUR TONGUE HAS DIFFERENT AREAS TO DETECT SALTY, SWEET AND SOUR TASTES

In the past, the 'tongue map' was a common feature of many school library books about the human body. It featured a tongue divided neatly into areas, each of which could register only one taste: the tip of the tongue detected sweet tastes, sides of the tongue detected salty and sour tastes, and the back of the tongue detected bitter tastes. It was all neat and tidy but very, very wrong.

Since the 1970s, scientific research has shown that taste buds are groups of test receptors bundled together on tiny bumps, called papillae, on your tongue and the roof of your mouth. These detect a range of tastes and are not clearly grouped as the tongue map indicates. You start life with up to 10,000 taste buds, which are replaced regularly by your body – but as you age, not all buds are renewed.

ERROR 3 YOU CAN TICKLE YOURSELF

Oh, no you can't... not properly. You can touch your palm lightly with a finger and might get a slight shiver, but you cannot twitch, giggle and beg yourself to stop by tickling your most ticklish parts. Scientists think this is because your brain knows where all of your body parts are and what they are doing, and tickling needs some element of unexpectedness or surprise to work.

THE PAINFUL TRUTH

ERROR 1 — URINE CAN SOOTHE THE PAIN OF A JELLYFISH STING

Jellyfish are found in all of the world's oceans. There are many species of these brainless creatures, from specimens a few millimetres long to giants of the sea. The Nomura's jellyfish has a body, called a bell, measuring more than 90cm in diameter. Its total weight is in excess of 100kg.

Jellyfish have tiny stinging cells in their tentacles to stun or paralyze their prey before they eat them. Called nematocysts, these stingers can be painful and sometimes deadly dangerous to humans as well. The advice from the Red Cross and other organizations is to get out of the sea as quickly as possible to avoid further stings and seek medical attention.

Urine was once thought to help soothe a sting because it can contain ammonia, but the amount in each person's urine varies and may be nowhere near enough to help. In addition, with some species of jellyfish, weeing on the sting might make things worse, causing other stinging cells to fire. To be on the safe side, keep your swimmers on and get first aid immediately!

ERROR 2 · WARTS CAN BE CAUGHT FROM TOADS

Many toads look warty but those lumps and bumps on their backs are actually glands, which produce a poisonous mucus that helps the toad to defend itself against predators. Toads may also urinate when picked up by humans – so there are two good reasons not to handle these amphibians, but catching warts is certainly not a third. Human warts are caused by the human papilloma virus (HPV), which has more than 100 different strains (varieties). It is a human-only virus and usually enters the body through broken skin, such as a cut or graze, not from toads or other animals. So that myth can hop off!

ERROR 3 · RABIES IS SPREAD TO HUMANS ONLY BY DOG BITES

Sometimes things are not just wrong, they're wrong and wrong again! The statement above is incorrect on two counts. Rabies is a disease that affects the human nervous system and brain, and can cause death if not treated quickly and effectively. It is transmitted in the saliva of animals, so a rabid dog doesn't have to bite you in order to infect you. Its drool just has to enter your body. An infected dog might lick a scratch or cut on human skin, or the saliva might reach the mucus membranes in the nose, mouth or throat. But dogs are not always the culprits. Most mammals can infect humans with the disease. The most common rabies transmitters – other than dogs – include bats, monkeys, racoons, skunks, foxes and cats.

SPREADING LIES

ERROR 1 SPANISH FLU CAME FROM SPAIN

In 1918, the first reports of a new and devastating wave of influenza (flu) emerged. World War I (1914-18) was about to end and the countries engaged in battle had strict rules on what their newspapers could and could not write about. Spain, however, remained neutral throughout the war and its papers were the first to report in detail about this deadly 'pandemic' (a big spread of infectious disease).

Even though it was initially known by other names, including 'three-day fever' and *La Grippe* (in French), the name Spanish Flu or *La gripe Española* (in Spanish) stuck. Today, most scientists refer to it as the 1918 Influenza Pandemic.

So where did Spanish flu really come from? Well, we're not certain – but it was definitely not Spain. Some researchers think it originated in China, while the first known cases occurred in a US military outpost in Fort Riley, Kansas, in March 1918. But the disease spread widely, hitting every continent around the world as a second wave, more deadly than the first, ran riot. Between 20 and 35 per cent of the entire world's population became ill, and 20–50 million people died – more than all the military deaths from fighting during World War I put together.

LEPROSY IS A DISEASE FOUND ONLY IN HUMANS THAT CAUSES PARTS OF THE BODY TO FALL OFF

ERROR 2

Leprosy (also known as Hansen's disease) is caused by the slow-growing bacteria *Mycobacterium leprae*. If untreated, it can cause nerve damage, leading to people losing feeling in parts of their body, suffering injuries and infection, and also blindness. Contrary to popular belief, it does not cause parts of the body to drop off, though a severe leprosy sufferer may be disfigured.

Many people consider leprosy to affect only humans, but it is a disease found in several other animals around the world, including the common chimpanzee, the sooty mangabey monkey in Africa and the nine-banded armadillo in the USA. This species of armadillo is currently being studied by scientists, as it may also be able to transmit the disease to humans.

MOSQUITOES HELP SPREAD THE HIV VIRUS

ERROR 3

This is a popular statement found on Internet forums and websites that should really know better. There is absolutely no truth in this vicious, viral rumour. Mosquitoes can transmit malaria, dengue fever and some other diseases, but why not HIV – the virus that causes AIDS (acquired immune deficiency syndrome) – in humans? The reason is to do with the HIV virus itself. It cannot survive inside a mosquito to reproduce and multiply like the malaria parasite does. When a mosquito feeds on the blood of an HIV-infected person, the HIV virus is destroyed as it is broken down in the mosquito's digestive system.

A PLAGUE OF ERRORS

ERROR 1

THE PLAGUE WAS AN HISTORIC DISEASE, CAUSED BY RATS, WHICH NO LONGER EXISTS

History books are full of stories of this dreaded disease. Although rats hastened its spread, they were not the direct cause. The lethal culprit was the *Yersinia pestis* bacteria transmitted by insects – particularly fleas, which are found on rats and other animals.

The first known major outbreak of 'bubonic' plague (the most lethal strain of plague) was known as the Plague of Justinian. It began in Egypt – or possibly southern Turkey – in about 541ce, and spread through large parts of Europe and the Middle East. It is believed to have killed more than 33 per cent of Europe's entire population. The Black Death was the ultimate plague pandemic. It killed as many as 75 million people by 1400, wiping out whole towns and stripping Europe of 30–60 per cent of its entire human population.

The Black Death wasn't the last of the plague. It has never died out: there have been major outbreaks in Italy (1629–31), London (1665–66) and Vienna in Austria (1679). Its third major pandemic began in the Yunnan province of China in 1855, spread to India and killed about 12 million people in those two countries. Plague struck San Francisco, USA, in the 1900s, and the World Health Organization reports that 1,000–3,000 cases of plague still occur every year, worldwide. Most occur in Africa, but plague cases were also reported in Peru, South America, in 2010 and New Mexico, USA, in 2011.

DISEASES NEVER GET TOTALLY WIPED OUT

ERROR 2

Plague sounds scary, but don't panic. Cases are very rare and medical knowledge has advanced so that many patients can be treated and can recover. But does this mean all the diseases that existed in the past are still lurking? In a word... no!

In 2011, the United Nations announced that rinderpest – a disease that affects cattle, buffalo, antelope, deer and giraffes – had been wiped out. About 30 years earlier, smallpox (a major killer of humans) was also eradicated. Smallpox originated more than 3,000 years ago and, during the 18th

century, killed one in every ten children in both France and Sweden. There was no effective treatment for the disease, which also took the lives of famous kings and queens including Pharaoh Ramesses V, King Louis XV of France, Tsar Peter II of Russia, Emperor Joseph I of Austria and King Luis I of Spain.

In 1966, there were 10 to 15 million cases of smallpox in more than 50 countries, with more than 1.5 million deaths from the disease. Huge efforts to protect people with a vaccine resulted in it being eradicated by 1980. No new cases have been reported since.

DEAD ENDS

ERROR 1 HAIR AND FINGERNAILS CONTINUE TO GROW AFTER DEATH

If you think this is true, you're dead wrong. You've been watching too many horror movies.

Fingernails grow at the rate of roughly one-tenth of a millimetre a day. They stop growing after death. Dead bodies dehydrate (lose water) over time. It is this process that gives the impression of hair and nail growth, because the flesh on hands and fingers shrinks and pulls back as it dries out. So, if you reopened a coffin after a time you would see the same-sized fingernails sitting on a smaller, shorter finger – giving the impression of longer nails. It's the same case with hair – the scalp shrinks and exposes more of the existing hair, making it look a little longer than before. Creepy!

ERROR 2 DEAD BODIES STAY STIFF

When somebody dies, their body goes through a number of changes. Few of them are pleasant. There's *pallor mortis*, in which blood stops flowing through vessels near the skin's surface, making it look more pale – as well as *algor mortis*, in which the body's temperature lowers after death. *Rigor mortis* is the stiffness of a body caused by a loss of a substance called adenosine triphosphate (ATP) from the muscles. It begins a few hours after death, reaching its peak after about 12 hours. *Rigor mortis* then fades away, leaving the body limp and floppy 48–72 hours after death. Grimaces reported on dead people's faces are often just the result of facial muscles tightening during *rigor mortis*.

MORE PEOPLE ARE ALIVE TODAY THAN HAVE EVER LIVED

ERROR 3

The last century has seen a global population explosion. According to the USA's Census Bureau, it passed 7,000 million people in March 2012 for the first time. In 1900, there were only about 1,600 million. But does that mean all the people alive today number more than all the people who have ever lived in the past? A lot of fact books and magazine columns reckon so. However, we reckon that they must have failed maths at school.

There are no clear records of births and deaths stretching back to the start of human history, but a glance at some estimates of world populations in the past prove that this 'fact' simply doesn't add up.

Let's take just one example we can do ourselves. The world population was about 200–300 million people in 1CE, which slowly rose to 500 million by 1600CE. During this long period, most people had a life expectancy of less than 50 years, so each century would contain two or more different generations of people. If you multiply each of the thirty-two 50-year periods between 1 and 1600CE by even a low average of 250 million people, you get 8,000 million – more than are on the planet today. And that's before we add the thousands of millions of people who have lived and died since 1600CE, and the hundreds of millions who lived before 1CE.

Demographics is the study of populations, including who people are, where they are and how their numbers change over time. In 2002, a demographer at the Population Reference Bureau used historical population charts to estimate the number of people who have ever lived at 106,000 million – making the numbers alive today just six per cent of those who've lived.

IN THE TIME IT TAKES YOU TO READ THIS SENTENCE, ABOUT 50,000 OF YOUR BODY'S CELLS WILL DIE AND BE REPLACED BY NEW ONES.

A BLOCK OF HUMAN BONE ABOUT THE SIZE OF A MATCHBOX CAN SUPPORT AS MUCH AS NINE TONNES OF WEIGHT – MORE THAN SOME FORMS OF CONCRETE CAN SUPPORT.

STRETCHED OUT, YOUR BODY'S BLOOD VESSELS WOULD COVER MORE THAN 90,000KM IN LENGTH. THAT'S ENOUGH TO CIRCLE THE EARTH SEVERAL TIMES WITH EASE.

THE SULABH INTERNATIONAL MUSEUM OF TOILETS IS A REAL-LIFE MUSEUM FOUND IN NEW DELHI, INDIA, WITH DOZENS OF CHAMBER POTS, COMMODES, TOILETS AND OTHER LAVATORIAL DEVICES.

YOUR HEART PUMPS APPROXIMATELY 7,500 LITRES OF BLOOD AROUND YOUR BODY EVERY DAY, AND IT BEATS AN ESTIMATED 35 MILLION TIMES PER YEAR.

MORE THAN 80 PER CENT OF THE WORLD'S SPINACH, SOME 17 MILLION TONNES, IS GROWN IN CHINA. SPINACH IS A QUICK GROWER AND CAN BE HARVESTED IN LESS THAN SIX WEEKS AFTER IT IS PLANTED.

SEDLEC OSSUARY IS A SMALL ROMAN CATHOLIC CHAPEL IN THE CZECH REPUBLIC. IT CONTAINS THE BONES OF MORE THAN 40,000 PEOPLE. MANY OF THE BONES HAVE BEEN FASHIONED INTO FURNITURE AND DECORATIONS INSIDE THE BUILDING.

RIDICULOUS! BUT TRUE...

ANIMAL ERRORS

CHAPTER 2

When British naturalist George Shaw was sent a stuffed, duck-billed platypus from Australia in 1799, he thought someone had sewn a duck's beak onto another creature as a joke. But the duck-billed mammal, which lays eggs and has webbed feet, was no hoax. Neither are the plants that eat insects or the squid that's 14m long with an eye the size of your dinner plate.

The natural world continues to surprise us. Every year, new species of plants or animals are discovered, with a staggering 19,233 found in 2009 alone. And that's not all. Every year more and more research reveals further amazing revelations about many plants and creatures and how they live and survive, forcing naturalists to revise their beliefs and facts about different species.

So, if you've ever been told that the blue whale is the biggest living thing on the planet, that bats are blind or ostriches stick their head in the sand, then you've been had, pure and simple. These animal errors are errors indeed. They are simply... not... true.

BEASTLY BELIEFS

 ERROR 1

THE BIGGEST LIVING THING IS THE BLUE WHALE

Let's make no whalebones about it, the blue whale is an absolute whopper. Capable of growing up to 30m in length and weighing 180 tonnes, it is so large that its heart is the size of a small car. To grow to that size, baby blue whales drink as much as 400 litres of milk from their mothers each day.

The blue whale is the biggest ever mammal and the largest animal on Earth, but there are living things that are much larger.

The plant kingdom includes much bigger things. Hyperion is a coastal redwood tree in California, USA, and at 115.61m in height it is the world's tallest tree. The famous General Sherman is a giant *Sequoia* tree with a circumference of more than 31m at its base, a height of 83.5m and a total weight of 1,488 tonnes. That's some chunky trunkies! Another contender could blow whales and giant trees out of the water... and it's a fungus. *Armillaria solidipes*, also called the honey fungus, is known for its large, capped mushrooms that grow above the forest floor. The rest of the fungus spreads out beneath the forest floor. One specimen, found in the USA's Malheur National Forest, Oregon, extends over an area of between 880 and 965 hectares – that's more than 1,500 football pitches! Scientists have yet to work out whether this fungus is a single living thing or has split into separate fungi.

ERROR 2 — ALL IVORY COMES FROM ELEPHANTS

The biggest animal on land is the elephant, no question. And when you think of ivory, you probably think of an elephant's tusks. But the truth of the matter is that ivory refers to the dentine that is found in the teeth or tusks of a wide range of creatures, including you (in your teeth – we don't expect you have tusks). Before there were plastics, strong yet lightweight ivory was in demand as a material to make lots of items, from the white keys of pianos to ornaments and false teeth. Ivory was obtained by hunting not only elephants but also hippos, walruses, wild pigs and narwhals (toothed, tusked whales).

ERROR 3 — RHINO HORNS ARE MADE OF MATTED HAIR

The second biggest land mammal after the elephant is the white rhinoceros. The largest white rhinoceros can reach a length of 4.4m and would destroy your bathroom scales, weighing a gut-busting 4,500kg. These hefty beasts are famous for the large horn on the end of their snout, which is made of a protein called keratin – the same substance found in horse's hooves and your fingernails. But it is NOT hair matted and stuck together, as many sources suggest. Computer scans of rhino horns have revealed that they also contain dense deposits of calcium, which gives them their strength, as well as melanin, the same substance that gives your skin its colour.

ANATOMICALLY INCORRECT

ERROR 1 · CENTIPEDES HAVE 100 LEGS

If you've been told this, someone's been pulling your leg. Despite their name, meaning 'hundred-footed', no centipede has been found with precisely 100 legs, though more than 3,000 species have been examined and catalogued.

Every species of centipede found so far has an odd number of pairs of legs. Some species have as few as 15 pairs, while the European centipede (*Himantarum gabrielis*) has 177 pairs – that's 354 legs in total. Centipedes can sometimes even regrow legs lost after an attack from a bird or another predator.

By the way, the largest known centipede, the Amazonian giant, can grow to 30cm in length and eats lizards, frogs and – incredibly – bats. Yet, despite being a whopper of the centipede world, it has only 21 or 23 pairs of legs.

ERROR 2 — CAMELS STORE WATER IN THEIR HUMPS

Don't get the hump, but this is false. Camels are built to survive many days without water and up to three weeks without food. The secret is in the hump on their back — or, in the case of Bactrian camels, the pair of humps. Each big lump doesn't hold water — it's a huge store of up to 35kg of fat. The body of a very hungry camel converts this fat into energy.

So, how can camels go without water for so long without a giant water tank? Camels have many adaptations for life in hot, dry desert areas. Their red blood cells are oval-shaped rather than round, allowing them to flow even when a camel is dehydrated (lacking water). Also, their kidneys and intestines are very efficient, recovering almost every drop of water from their digestive system. Their nostrils can even trap and recycle much of the water vapour in their breath as they breathe out.

ERROR 3 — OSTRICHES STICK THEIR HEAD IN THE SAND

The old myth goes that ostriches are so stupid that, when in danger, they stick their head in the sand rather than run away. But this would be very odd behaviour for a tall creature with sharp vision, able to spot trouble from a distance. When danger looms in the form of a lion, leopard or hyena, ostriches use their long legs to sprint away at speeds of up to 70km/h.

So where does the myth come from? In the African plains where ostriches live, the landscape is mostly dirt and scrubland, not sand. Sometimes ostriches bend down to turn their eggs on the ground or to swallow pebbles, which help them to digest their food as they have no teeth. From a distance, with heat hazes causing the ground to shimmer and appear fuzzy, it may look like an ostrich's head is disappearing below ground.

FALSE MOVES

ERROR 1 BEARS CANNOT RUN DOWNHILL

Grrrr. This myth makes some naturalists and wilderness guides as angry as a grizzly with a thorn in its paw. It's a potentially dangerous one as well, with bear attacks occurring every year.

Yes, okay... bears' front paws are shorter and less powerful than their back paws – BUT, if they run down a slope, bears don't fall over. Bears run up and down hills and slopes all the time, and they can do it at speed. They are surprisingly nimble, agile and fast creatures for their size. Most bears can run at speeds of more than 40km/h – about the same as a 100m sprint world record holder moving at peak speed – meaning that you're unlikely to outpace them over a distance.

WHEN IT COMES TO JUMPING, THE FROGHOPPER CAN JUMP MORE THAN 100 TIMES ITS OWN HEIGHT.

ERROR 2 ELEPHANTS ARE THE ONLY ANIMALS THAT CANNOT JUMP

Some say elephants are far too heavy to jump. The heaviest elephants weigh about 10,900kg. Others say that elephants have no reason to jump because they can reach a lot of food with their large trunks, and they never have to leap over an obstacle to flee danger. All agree, though, that an elephant cannot jump. But there's a twist. There are other members of the animal kingdom that cannot jump, including three-toed sloths and molluscs such as clams and earthworms. The legs of rhinoceroses and hippopotamuses can all leave the ground momentarily while running, but neither of these two can jump properly from a standing start.

ERROR 3 CROCODILES RUN FASTER THAN PEOPLE

Much of the belief about crocodiles' speed comes from their sudden lunges. This often results in successful attacks – but it isn't running.

When it comes to real running, the Australian freshwater crocodile is the speed king. It actually gallops like a horse using its short, powerful legs. The fastest recorded speed is 17km/h. Most other crocs tend to slither on their bellies, so they are slower. According to the Crocodilian Biology Database, 12–14km/h is their maximum speed and this can be maintained only for short bursts. So most people, sprinting hard, can outrun a crocodile. But please don't try it or you might end up as croc food!

IF YOU COULD JUMP LIKE A FROGHOPPER, YOU COULD CLEAR A 150-M-TALL BUILDING!

COLOURFUL CHARACTERS

ERROR 1 — CHAMELEONS CHANGE COLOUR TO MATCH THEIR SURROUNDINGS

There are more than 100 species of chameleon. Most of these types of lizard can change the colour of their appearance in just 20 seconds. But if you thought they did it to camouflage themselves and hide, you'd be wrong.

Many chameleons, especially male ones, change colour to do the exact opposite of hiding. They're showing off to potential female mates by displaying their fanciest look. Some species become a rainbow of bright pinks, blues, purples and yellows with different colours on their head and eyelids.

Chameleons also change colour due to changes in light and temperature around them. In bright sunlight, many chameleons will turn lighter in colour. This helps to reflect sunlight.

If the weather turns cooler, they may change from a light green or yellow to a brown colour. Darker colours absorb more of the sun's energy and help cold-blooded chameleons stay warm.

ERROR 2 BULLS ARE ENRAGED BY THE COLOUR RED

You've seen it many times in films and cartoons – a character wearing scarlet or holding a red object while being chased by a furious bull. But the bull is not in a rage over the colour red.

Bulls are actually colour-blind. In bullfighting, you will see them charge at the matador's cape, which is red on one side. But the bull is angry because it has been teased, prodded and sometimes hurt by lances and sharp sticks dug into its body. The bulls aim for the cape because of its movement, not its colour. They will charge just as furiously at the inside of the cape, which is often coloured yellow.

ERROR 3 POLAR BEARS ARE WHITE

The skin of a polar bear is actually black. It has a close, insulating layer of fur and then, above that, a layer of what looks to be white hair. These 'guard hairs' make up the polar bear's protective outer layer and they are transparent (see-through). Each hair has a hollow core, which reflects and scatters the light hitting it, making it *appear* white.

BLACK OR VERY DARK GREY SKIN UNDERNEATH THE WHITE HAIR THAT FORMS THE STRIPES.

SENSELESS!

ERROR 1 — GOLDFISH HAVE A THREE-SECOND MEMORY

Goldfish have a three-second... what was that again? Imagine only remembering what you were doing or going to do for three seconds. You wouldn't get anything done! Fortunately, goldfish don't tend to have as packed a social and school life as you do, but doesn't such a short memory span smell fishy to you?

In 2008, Australian schoolboy Rory Stokes performed his own aquatic experiment, placing fish food beside a red LEGO® brick in his fish tank each day for three weeks. Then, he left the goldfish alone for a week before placing the red brick back in the tank. The goldfish swam straight back over to it, expecting food and proving it boasted a 604,800-second memory (60 seconds x 60 minutes x 24 hours x 7 days). Rory's research wasn't the only study on this popular pet. Goldfish at Israel's Institute of Technology were trained to recognize that a certain sound meant feeding time. They remembered the sound when it was played again five months later.

BATS ARE BLIND

You're batty if you believe this one! There are more than 1,100 species of bats, which come in two broad types – mega and micro. Megabats (*Megachiropterans*) are the bigger bats that eat fruit, nectar and sometimes small animals. They include flying foxes and fruit bats. They're most definitely not blind since they possess big eyes and large vision centres in their brain. They rely on their daylight vision to fly and, along with their sense of smell, find their food.

Microbats (*Microchiropterans*) tend to have small eyes, cannot see in colour, and use echolocation to navigate and hunt at night. They send out high-pitched sounds, which bounce off an object and come back. Bats detect the returning sounds and calculate how far they are from the object. All this goes on in a fraction of a second. Even with this super-sense microbats still rely on their eyesight, which scientists believe is sensitive in low light conditions, to avoid big objects and see across long distances.

PENGUINS FALL OVER BACKWARDS WHEN WATCHING PLANES FLY OVER THEM

Reported as far and wide as Mexico, the UK and India is the claim that penguins watch aircraft overhead so carefully that they lose their balance and topple over. Sounds comical – but if it were the case, it would be a big deal for some penguins who struggle to right themselves again after falling onto their backs.

Such was the interest in these claims that, in the year 2000, a team of researchers led by Dr Richard Stone of the British Antarctic Survey travelled to the island of South Georgia, near Antarctica. Here, they investigated the reaction of a colony of 1,000 king penguins to aircraft flying overhead. Some of the birds did watch the planes, and the whole colony went quieter than usual, but in the five weeks the researchers were present they didn't see a single penguin fall over backwards.

HAVE YOU HEARD...?

ERROR 1 SNAKE CHARMERS CHARM SNAKES WITH THEIR MUSIC

Once common in markets, town squares and bazaars of the Middle East, India and other Asian countries, snake charming has a long hisssss-tory and may have first begun in the time of the ancient Egyptians, more than 4,000 years ago.

A man plays a flute and sways, luring a large and sometimes deadly snake out of a basket. The cobra starts to sway, appearing to keep rhythm with the music. It looks amazing, but is something slippery afoot?

Many people think that charming cannot work because snakes are deaf. They don't have external ears like your lugholes, but they do have inner ear mechanisms and can sense low-frequency vibrations that run underground and sometimes through the air. However, they are deaf to the higher-pitched sound waves coming from the musical instrument. It is actually the moving of the charmer and the flute that captures the snake's attention and makes it sway back and forth.

ERROR 2 GIRAFFES CANNOT MAKE A SOUND

The tallest land creatures on the planet, giraffes can stand 5–6m in height. They have a 2-metre-long neck, with plenty of space for a set of vocal cords, but they don't have them. However, they can still make noises. Young giraffe calves make snorts and quiet mooing sounds, while adult giraffes will occasionally hiss, moan and bellow. When courting female giraffes, male bull giraffes sometimes make loud coughs to attract attention.

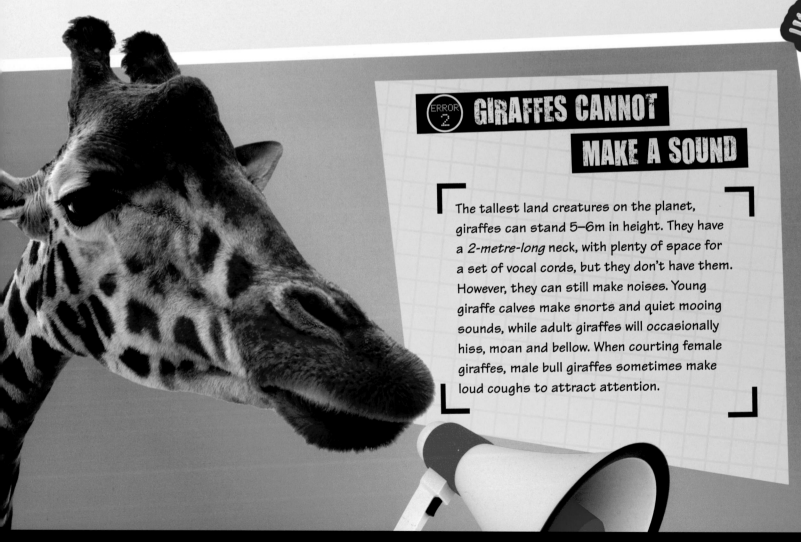

A GIRAFFE'S TONGUE IS ABOUT 50CM LONG, ENABLING IT TO GRASP HIGH BRANCHES AND GULP DOWN LEAVES.

ERROR 3
LOBSTERS SCREAM WHEN PLUNGED INTO BOILING WATER

Those of you of a nervous disposition, turn away now. Lobsters are cooked whole, usually by plunging them into a large pot of boiling water. Many people report noises that sound like small, high-pitched screams as a lobster is boiled. But lobsters have no way of making such a sound. They breathe through gills in a similar way to fish, and have no lungs or vocal cords. The sounds that some cooks report are most likely produced by air inside the lobster's shell escaping as it is plunged into the hot water.

AN ADULT GIRAFFE CAN EAT MORE THAN 30KG OF FOLIAGE A DAY. SLURP!

SURVIVAL STORIES

ERROR 1 SHARKS HAVE NO ENEMIES OTHER THAN HUMANS

Few creatures seem more terrifying than a shark, its jaws wide open, teeth glinting, and about to attack. Some sharks are spectacular predators, powering through the water equipped, in the great white shark's case, with up to 300 razor-sharp teeth.

But sharks can also be injured or preyed upon by other animals besides humans (who kill thousands of sharks every year). Killer whales, sperm whales and even dolphins will occasionally attack and kill sharks. Shark species also prey upon each other. The remains of eaten nurse sharks have been found in the stomachs of tiger sharks, while the smalleye hammerhead shark has been a snack for both bull sharks and great hammerheads.

ERROR 2 — TORTOISES ARE THE LONGEST-LIVING CREATURES

Some species of tortoise can live for 150 years or more. Jonathan, a Seychelles giant tortoise, is believed to be more than 180 years old. When he was born, in about 1832, William IV was Britain's king and the USA were on to only their seventh president.

But he's not the oldest of all. NOAA, the USA's National Oceanic and Atmospheric Administration, lists the rougheye rockfish as living for up to 205 years, while bowhead whales may be the oldest mammals (they live for up to 200 years). One type of clam, the ocean quahog, may live to between 225 and 400 years of age. Yet all these old-timers are eclipsed by Antarctic sponges – some of which are estimated at more than 1,500 years old – and by black corals, found in the Gulf of Mexico, which have been dated at 2,000 years old.

ERROR 3 — COLONIES OF LEMMINGS LEAP OFF CLIFFS TO THEIR DEATHS

Some lemmings are believed to migrate in large numbers from place to place, but do they commit mass suicide? Viewers of a 1958 Oscar-winning documentary film, called *White Wilderness,* were made to think so as they watched lemmings leap off a cliff into what the film's narrator said was the Arctic Ocean.

The truth is different. Lemmings have never been filmed leaping to their deaths in their native habitats. The film was shot in the landlocked Canadian province of Alberta, a place where lemmings aren't found, so small numbers were imported from the Arctic Circle. Instead of *choosing* to jump into the ocean, they were swept off a river bank by crew members with brooms. The film is shot in close-up, so you don't see the crew or realize there are only small numbers of lemmings.

INSECT BITES

ERROR 1 — THERE ARE 10 TIMES AS MANY INSECTS AS THERE ARE PEOPLE

That would be about 71 billion insects in total… way off. Our planet teems with insects, far more than you might realize or can count. Their numbers are HUGE.

Here's an example – a single soybean plant can support about 2,000 aphids and there can be as many as 400,000 plants in a hectare, so that's 800 million of just one type of insect in a single 100m by 100m field. One estimate from the Smithsonian Institute reckons there are some 10 trillion (10,000,000,000,000,000,000,000) insects on Earth. If this is divided by the total human population of 7.1 billion, it gives at least 1.4 billion insects for every person. Mind-blowing!

ERROR 2 — ALL MOSQUITOES BITE

Of course, some mosquitoes can strike, leaving you with an irritating spot. In parts of the world, they spread deadly diseases such as malaria and yellow fever. But male mosquitoes cannot bite at all. They feed on plant sap and nectar, and live shorter lives than female mosquitoes – they typically last a week, while females can live for up to a month. Not all female mosquitoes bite humans. Some bite only birds or amphibians. Even the female mosquitoes that target humans don't actually bite, because they have no jaw. Instead, they pierce the skin with their long, pointed mouthpart, called a proboscis. It has two tubes. One injects saliva, which contains substances that stop blood clotting, while the other draws out a little blood that gives the mosquito protein.

ERROR 3: COCKROACHES COULD SURVIVE A NUCLEAR BOMB ATTACK

Yes and no. It all depends on where the cockroach was standing, resting or scuttling as the bomb hit. Make no mistake about it – cockroaches are ridiculously tough. They can live without food for months, without air for almost an hour and can even survive for several weeks with their head chopped off! They are famous for being more resistant to harmful radiation than humans. In one experiment, German cockroaches were exposed to a similar level of radiation given off by the atomic bombs of World War II.

Some survived. These guys are hardcore. But a nuclear weapon today would generate higher levels of radiation, which it is doubtful cockroaches could survive. The physical force of the explosion would decimate any cockroaches close to the bomb's impact. Though cockroaches hate the cold and prefer warmer temperatures, they couldn't live with the extreme heat generated close to a nuclear weapon blast. Temperatures could reach as high as several million degrees Celsius. Simply scorching!

OF MAMMAL, BUT MORE THAN 900,000 SPECIES OF INSECT.

CANINE CONFLICTS

ERROR 1 DOGS SWEAT BY PANTING

As long as 14,000 years ago, dogs may have been the first type of animal that humans domesticated and brought into their homes.

Dogs have since become popular pets and faithful companions for millions of people, but do you know all the facts about your pooch? The skin under a dog's fur doesn't contain any sweat glands and dogs sweat only a tiny amount through the pads on the bottom of their paws.

They mostly cool off through the process of panting. This is when a dog opens its mouth, lets its tongue hang out and takes lots of breaths in through its nose and out through its mouth. As a result, moisture from its lungs, mouth and tongue evaporates into the air, and this helps the dog to cool down.

ERROR 2 A WAGGING TAIL MEANS A DOG IS HAPPY AND FRIENDLY

Not always. But many postal workers have been fooled into thinking this! Dog behaviour experts explain that a wagging tail can mean many things, from happiness and excitement at seeing their owner (or dinner) to agitation or fear when faced with a rival dog or other threat. Italian neuroscientists and vets at the universities of Bari and Trieste found that dogs tended to wag their tails more to the right of their backside when happy, and more to the left when feeling hostile or under threat.

ERROR 3: A DOG IS SICK WHEN ITS NOSE IS DRY

Most dogs' noses are cold and slightly wet to the touch because some of their tear glands empty onto their nose. A warm or dry nose doesn't necessarily mean that a dog is poorly, nor does a cold or wet nose guarantee that a dog is in great health. Canine noses may turn wetter, cooler, or drier and warmer throughout the day. The only accurate way to check a dog's health is with a thermometer. A healthy temperature ranges between about 38.3°C and 39.2°C.

ERROR 4: CHOCOLATE DOESN'T HARM DOGS

Yes it can. Chocolate is made from cocoa beans, which contain a substance called theobromine that can be extremely harmful to dogs. A large dose of theobromine can cause pooches to vomit, have heart problems, suffer seizures or even die. Choc drops made for dogs are very low in theobromine, but dark and baking chocolate – intended for humans – contain too much theobromine for dogs to consume.

HABITAT HOWLERS

ERROR 1 MOST WILD CAMELS LIVE IN AFRICA

Camels are called the 'ships of the desert', so you'd expect lots of them to live wild in Africa's Sahara desert or in parts of central Asia. But you're not even close...

Nearly all camels in Africa are domesticated in herds and used by humans for transportation, as well as for their milk and meat. Small herds of wild camels are found in the Gobi desert in China and Mongolia, but their total number is only about 1,000. In contrast, over in Oceania, there are at least one million camels roaming wild in the Australian outback. Camels were first introduced into Australia in large numbers in the 1860s. More than 10,000 camels were brought over initially to help explore the vast landmass and to transport supplies, until they were replaced by motor vehicles in the 20th century. Released into the wild, Aussie camels have multiplied in number. A 2001 study of camels in Australia's Northern Territory estimated that the camel population doubled once every eight years. A whole lot of humps!

ERROR 2 MOST TIGERS ARE FOUND IN INDIA

These beautiful big cats were once found throughout Asia, from Turkey and Russia through to India, Nepal, Southeast Asia and China. Their numbers have been slashed due to hunting and habitat destruction (clearing forests for logging, farming and new settlements). The World Wildlife Fund estimates that there are as few as 3,200 tigers left in the wild. India is home to the largest wild tiger population with about 1,400, but did you know there are more than 5,000 tigers in the USA? Most are not in zoos, but are kept as pets by individuals.

ERROR 3 PENGUINS LIVE ONLY IN ICE-COLD CLIMATES

You'll never see a penguin fleeing a polar bear as no penguins live in the Arctic Circle, where polar bears roam. Penguins are mostly found at the other end of the Earth, around the Antarctic Circle. Some species of penguins, though, live in far less chilly climates along the coasts of Chile, Australia and New Zealand. About 140,000 penguins live along the African coastlines of South Africa and Namibia. Meanwhile, straddling the middle of the Earth, 970km west of Ecuador, live the Galápagos penguins, in warm temperatures of 21–26°C.

OFF THE NORTHWEST COAST OF AFRICA, TO AUSTRALIA IN 1840.

EGGSTREMELY FOOLISH

ERROR 1 · ALL FISH LAY EGGS

Some fish not only lay eggs, they lay loads of them. A female Atlantic cod may lay as many as 4-6 million eggs in a single go (called a spawning), while the ocean sunfish or mola mola can lay up to 300 million!

Yet, not all species of fish lay eggs. Some create eggs that develop inside the mother's body and are born as live baby fish. Guppies, sawfish, pupfish, the Amazon molly and the cownose ray are all examples, as are many species of shark – including the fearsome great white shark. Some sharks, such as the shortfin mako and the grey nurse shark, hatch from their eggs while still inside their mother, and gain nourishment by eating up other eggs before they hatch. These are called intra-uterine cannibals!

Guppy

Shark

ERROR 2: A BABY BIRD OR BIRD EGG HANDLED BY A HUMAN WILL BE REJECTED BY ITS MOTHER

Was this false fact started by parents to make kids leave eggs and young birds alone? No one knows. Apart from scavengers, such as vultures, most birds have a limited sense of smell and may not detect a human's scent. It is unlikely to stop them caring for their young anyway.

However, eggs and baby birds should be left alone. Young birds on the ground may be learning to fly, so they should not be put back in their nest. Many bird species are under threat, so collecting their eggs is illegal in a lot of countries.

Echidna

Bird's egg

ERROR 3: ALL MAMMALS GIVE BIRTH TO LIVE YOUNG

Just as not all fish lay eggs, not every mammal gives birth to live young. The monotremes of Australia and New Guinea are five species of mammal that lay eggs. They include the duck-billed platypus and four species of echidnas. Leathery-shelled eggs form in the mother platypus and stay there for 28 days, absorbing nutrients before they are laid in the burrow. They take another 10 days to hatch into tiny, hairless babies, which feed on the mother's milk. In an echidna, usually only one egg is produced at a time. The mother rolls the egg into a temporary pouch in her body, which develops when she becomes pregnant. The egg takes about 10 days to hatch.

SEEDS OF DOUBT

ERROR 1 PEANUTS ARE NUTS

Some foods are not quite what you think they are. Did you know that many ice creams contain a seaweed extract called carrageenan, which helps to keep them creamy? But peanuts suffering an identity crisis? Are we nuts??

Botanists (scientists who study plant biology) define nuts as fruits in a hard shell, which grow above ground, often on trees or bushes such as the chestnut or hazel. Peanuts, in contrast, grow underground in pods, which means they are 'legumes' – a family of plants that includes peas, beans, soy, lentils and alfalfa. A peanut plant flowers above ground and then the stalk starts to bend and grow down, penetrating the soil. Later, it develops pods containing the plant's seed – the peanut – under the soil. Millions of tonnes of peanuts are grown worldwide, and about 540 peanuts are used to make a typical jar of peanut butter.

ERROR 2 TOMATOES ARE VEGETABLES

From salads and sauces to salsas and soups, tomatoes are eaten as a savoury dish. So, surely they are vegetables? Afraid not. While treated as a vegetable by cooks and chefs, science knows they are a fruit. More specifically, a berry.

Tomatoes, like other fruits classified as berries, develop from a single ovary (part of the female reproductive organs of a flowering plant) and contain the seeds of a plant. Producing edible fruits is a common way for plants to disperse their seeds: the fruits are eaten and passed through the digestive systems of animals. Tomatoes are much lower in sugar than most other fruits, which is why you don't eat them in a dessert. But tomatoes are not the only fruit mistaken for vegetables – scientifically speaking, cucumbers, squash and pumpkins are also fruits.

ORANGES ARE THE BEST NATURAL SOURCE OF VITAMIN C

A typical orange contains about 70 milligrams (mg) of vitamin C. This equals approximately 53mg of vitamin C per 100 grams of the fruit. While this is higher than the vitamin C in grapefruit (30mg per 100g) and mangoes (28mg), it is lower than that in strawberries (57mg per 100g) and kiwi fruit (93mg per 100g). All of them are beaten by blackcurrants, which have 200mg of vitamin C per 100g.

What's more, it's not just other fruits that contain more vitamin C than oranges. Broccoli (80mg per 100g), Brussels sprouts (90mg per 100g) and red bell peppers (190mg per 100g) all trounce oranges for vitamin C content.

THIAMINE (VITAMIN B1), POTASSIUM AND FIBRE – ALL ESSENTIALS FOR A HEALTHY BODY.

LEAFY LIES

ERROR 1

ALL PLANTS PRODUCE ENERGY THROUGH PHOTOSYNTHESIS

Many biology books tell us that plants are the only living things on Earth capable of making their own food through the process of photosynthesis. Chlorophyll (a substance found in plant cells) enables plants to convert carbon dioxide and water, using light energy from the Sun, into plant food and oxygen.

This is all very well, but there are a number of plants that don't have any chlorophyll. About 400 species of flowering plant, including pinedrops, the Indian pipe or corpse plant, broomrape and certain species of orchids, are 'myco-heterotrophs'. These are plants that get their food not from photosynthesis but from growing as parasites and obtaining their nutrients from fungi. Other plants, such as mistletoe, do perform some photosynthesis but not enough to sustain themselves. They rely on becoming a 'partial parasite' – growing on other plants and taking food and nutrients from them.

⊘ ERROR 2 MOSS GROWS ONLY ON THE NORTH-FACING SIDES OF TREES

Outdoor enthusiasts and survival experts suggest this idea as a great way to navigate if you've lost your compass or GPS receiver. Factually, however, it is THEY who have really lost their way.

The claim is based on the idea that mosses need moisture to flourish, and so prefer to be out of direct sunlight, growing mostly on the side of tree trunks facing north – the direction that is most out of the Sun. But this doesn't work for half the planet. South of the Equator, it is north-facing surfaces that receive the most sunlight. Even in Earth's northern half, or hemisphere, mosses can be found growing on all sides of a tree – especially if the forest receives a lot of rainfall, has a dense canopy of leaves to block out some sunlight, or if the north-facing sides of trees are in the shadow of other trees.

⊘ ERROR 3 TULIPS COME FROM THE NETHERLANDS

This popular flower is grown from bulbs, and the Netherlands are the centre of the tulip industry, producing about 3 billion (3,000,000,000) bulbs every year. But tulips did not originate on Dutch soil. Botanists believe that tulips originated in central Asia as a wild flower and now grow naturally in some parts of northern Africa and as far east as China. They were first cultivated possibly by the Turkish Ottoman empire, centuries before they reached western Europe and cities such as Vienna and Amsterdam, from the middle of the 16th century onwards.

THE NETHERLANDS

EUROPE

AUSTRIA

TURKEY

IT IS CLAIMED THAT PEOPLE EXCHANGED HORSES AND EVEN THEIR HOMES FOR A SINGLE BULB.

3M

JURASSIC LARK

ERROR 1 — THE JURASSIC ERA'S MOST DEADLY DINOSAUR WAS THE T-REX

We're not doubting *Tyrannosaurus*'s status as a truly deadly dinosaur. *T-Rex* was a serious killer, but it came late to the dinosaur party.

2M

The Jurassic era was a period of geological time starting about 199.6 million years ago and lasting for approximately 45 million years. Many dinosaurs lived during this time, but *Tyrannosaurus* wasn't one of them. More than 75 million years passed after the end of the Jurassic period before *T-Rex* arrived on the scene, about 67 million years ago. What a latecomer!

While we're talking about *T-Rex*, you should know that it wasn't the largest carnivorous dinosaur either. *Spinosaurus*, a monster dinosaur living in north Africa between 112 and 97 million years ago, is believed to be larger. Its estimated length ranges from 12.6 to 18m, with a weight of 7–20 tonnes. The largest *T-Rex* probably measured about 12.8m in length and weighed between 5.5 and 6.8 tonnes.

HUMAN MALE

1M

TURKEY

ERROR 2 — VELOCIRAPTOR WERE LARGE DINOSAURS FROM CENTRAL AMERICA

In the *Jurassic Park* films, large *Velociraptor* stole the show by terrifying and attacking humans. Real-life raptors living about 75 million years ago were not the size of a grizzly bear, as the film suggests. In truth, they were the size of a well-fed turkey: they stood less than a metre tall, but had a long tail measuring up to 2m. Palaeontologists estimate that they weighed 15kg at the most. The first real *Velociraptor* fossil was found in 1923 in Mongolia's Gobi desert. More partial or complete skeletons have since been recovered, all from Mongolia, China and Central Asia. This is a long way from the coast of Central America – the park's location in the films. Like turkeys, raptors had hollow bones and were covered in feathers.

0M

VELOCIRAPTOR

TYRANNOSAURUS REX

CRUSAFONTIA

FRUITAFOSSOR

ERROR 3 — MAMMALS EVOLVED AFTER THE DINOSAURS DIED OUT

With all those bad boys around, you wouldn't want to be a small, furry mammal during the dinosaur age, but mammals did exist at this time. Fossils of the mammal Fruitafossor, for example, have been found in North America, dating from the late Jurassic era (about 150 million years ago). The squirrel-like Crusafontia, first found in Portugal, lived about 110 million years ago. Mammals in the dinosaur period were mostly small and fed on plants, insects and lizards. Many could scurry up trees if danger loomed.

SPACE DISGRACE

ERROR 1 NO EARTH CREATURE CAN SURVIVE IN SPACE

Space is a seriously hostile place for living things. With none of Earth's atmosphere to shield you from the Sun, you'd be facing lethal temperature swings. There's no air, oxygen or water in space either – and if that is not enough, bursts of powerful radiation from the Sun could prove deadly in seconds. Surely, survival for any length of time would be simply impossible. Well, you'd think so...

One unusual little creature has lived in space, unprotected, and survived. A tardigrade, also known as a water bear, is a tiny creature – between 0.1 and 1.5mm long – with a barrel-shaped body and eight stubby legs. On Earth, tardigrades live mostly in water or wet mosses and lichens, but can suspend many of their body's functions and survive when thrown into really extreme environments. And it doesn't get much more extreme than the time when more than 3,000 tardigrades were launched on board a *Foton-M3* spacecraft from Baikonur

Cosmodrome in Kazakhstan. Their 2007 mission was called TARDIS (TARDigrades In Space) and it exposed them to the deadly conditions of space for 12 days.

Amazingly, many of the 3,000 water bears survived, and some were even able to breed as normal and lay eggs. In 2011, more tardigrades were sent into space and taken on board the International Space Station – as part of the Italian Space Agency's Project BIOKIS – to learn more about how they withstand the hardships of space.

LAIKA THE DOG WAS THE FIRST ANIMAL SENT INTO SPACE

ERROR 2

You may have heard of Laika, a stray dog found on the streets of Moscow and sent into space in 1957 on board *Sputnik 2*, the second spacecraft to orbit the Earth. Poor Laika was launched on a one-way ticket as the *Sputnik 2* craft was not designed to be safely recovered. She died in space a number of hours after the launch.

But she wasn't the first creature in space. She wasn't even the first dog from Russia to travel into space. Six years earlier, a Russian *R1* rocket carried two dogs, Dezik and Tsygan, to an altitude of about 110km above the Earth's surface, from which they were safely recovered. Before these dogs came a rhesus monkey called Albert II who, in 1949, travelled to a height of 134km on board a *V2* rocket modified by American scientists. Two years before Albert's trip into space, a small collection of *Drosophila* fruit flies was put on board another *V2* rocket and launched from White Sands in New Mexico, USA. These were the first space travellers from planet Earth.

WOLVES HOWL AT THE MOON

ERROR 3

This nugget of nature knowledge really is a howler. Many studies of wolf behaviour all agree that wolves don't howl at that shining orb or crescent in the sky. What they're actually doing is communicating with other wolves over long distances – sometimes as far as 9km away. Wolves tend to be more active at night, which is why you're more likely to hear their howling in the dark. They do tilt their head skywards, but only to help their howls to travel further.

WHEN THEY STAYED ON BOARD THE *SKYLAB* SPACE STATION IN 1973.

A GIANT ANTEATER'S TONGUE CAN FLICK IN AND OUT OF ITS MOUTH 150 TIMES A MINUTE. A LARGE AND VERY HUNGRY ANTEATER CAN GOBBLE UP MORE THAN 20,000 ANTS OR TERMITES IN A SINGLE DAY.

GIRAFFES HAVE THE SAME NUMBER OF NECK BONES AS HUMANS. IT'S JUST THAT EACH OF THESE VERTEBRAE ARE MUCH, MUCH LONGER THAN OURS.

'TOMMASO' STARTED LIFE AS A STRAY CAT BEFORE BEING BEFRIENDED BY ITALIAN MILLIONAIRESS MARIA ASSUNTA. WHEN ASSUNTA DIED IN 2011, SHE LEFT HER ENTIRE FORTUNE OF ALMOST £10 MILLION TO TOMMASO, WHO IS NOW THE WORLD'S RICHEST MOGGIE.

WHEN THE DOMINANT FEMALE IN A GROUP OF CLOWNFISH (ALSO KNOWN AS ANEMONEFISH) DIES, ONE OF THE LARGEST MALE FISHES TURNS FEMALE AND WILL EVENTUALLY SPAWN EGGS THAT HATCH INTO NEW FISH.

CAMELS HAVE THREE PAIRS OF EYELIDS. THE FIRST TWO PAIRS (THE UPPER AND LOWER EYELIDS) BOTH HAVE EYELASHES TO KEEP DUST AWAY FROM THE EYES. THE THIRD IS A PAIR OF THIN MEMBRANES THAT KEEP THE EYES MOIST AND CAN BE SEEN THROUGH (WHILE CLOSED) DURING A SANDSTORM.

SNAKES CANNOT SLINK BACKWARDS. THEY CAN PERFORM QUICK, SHARP U-TURNS TO CHANGE DIRECTION, BUT THEY CANNOT SLITHER IN REVERSE.

A LARGE OAK TREE CAN ABSORB ENOUGH WATER FROM THE GROUND IN A SINGLE DAY TO FILL SEVEN BATHTUBS.

ACCORDING TO THE NATURAL HISTORY MUSEUM IN LONDON, UK, 80 PER CENT OF THE CALORIES CONSUMED BY THE WORLD'S HUMAN POPULATION COMES FROM JUST SIX TYPES OF PLANT: RICE, WHEAT, MAIZE, POTATOES, SWEET POTATOES AND CASSAVA.

SCIENCE SLIP-UPS

CHAPTER 3

Science isn't a closed book. What we know is always changing as a result of new discoveries, research and theories. This can make some predictions from respected scientists and experts look foolish – fast.

Scientist Lord Kelvin found absolute zero, investigated heat, and pioneered telecommunications. But he also doubted X-rays or radio would ever work. In 1902 he stated, "No aeroplane will ever be practically successful." That was a year before the Wright Brothers' aircraft flew. In 1934 Albert Einstein said, "There is not the slightest indication that nuclear energy will ever be obtainable." Nuclear power now supplies 13 per cent of the world's electricity needs.

Not all of science remains accurate for ever and not all scientists get it right all of the time. Turn the page to see flaws in physics, trip-ups in technology and myths about matter and chemistry.

FLAWED PHYSICS

(ERROR 1) MASS AND WEIGHT ARE THE SAME

Physics is a tricky old science, full of complicated laws and principles. It is very easy to get one of these scientific facts wrong, and a classic gaff is to mistake weight for mass.

The mass of an object is how much stuff or matter it contains. This can be measured in grams (g) and kilograms (kg) and is a property of the object. So, a brick that has a mass of 1kg always has that mass whether it is on Earth, plonked on Mars or lobbed into space.

Weight is different. It is the force caused by gravity pulling down on the mass of an object. If the amount of gravity changes, then the weight of the object changes. For example, if you had a weight of 30kg on Earth, you would weigh just over 27kg on Venus, which has fractionally less gravity than Earth, and only 11.3kg on Mercury, which has much weaker gravity than Earth. In contrast, Jupiter has about two-and-a-half times as much gravity as Earth, so you would weigh 75kg there. But your mass would remain as 30kg.

In the days of yore, before science got going properly, people thought weight and mass were the same thing. So, then and now, the same units are usually used for both: kilograms etc. In actual fact, since weight is a force, its unit should be the 'newton', and physicists do use newtons to measure weight.

ERROR 2 COINS DROPPED FROM THE TOP OF TALL BUILDINGS CAN TRAVEL FAST ENOUGH TO KILL

This myth has long haunted cities that have towering skyscrapers. When completed in 1931, New York City's Empire State Building was the tallest building in the world. It held the record for 40 years. A coin dropped from the top of this skyscraper would increase speed for the first few seconds of its fall, but the resistance of the air would soon stop this increase. The coin would then continue to fall down at its so-called 'terminal' velocity, maybe at about 160km/h. What it does when it hits someone on the ground depends on this speed and on the mass of the coin: a small one, such as a US penny (1c) is only about 2.5g, and that means it could give that person only a nasty tap. In contrast, a much heavier, streamlined bullet fired from a gun can reach speeds of well over 1,000km/h – and is likely to do a LOT more damage than a coin if it hits someone.

ERROR 3 THINGS EXPAND AS THEY GET HOTTER

It's one of the first things you learn in science class. If you heat most materials, they expand to take up more space. This is the reason why, for example, there are small gaps left between railway tracks, to allow for the steel rails to swell up a little when they get hot.

But this principle of thermal expansion doesn't actually work for every single material. At very low temperatures, carbon fibres and silicon expand only when they're cooled, not when they're heated. Water, too, can take up less room when it is warmed up from its frozen state (ice). If an ice cube tray, with each of its moulds full, is taken out of the freezer and left to warm up, the ice will turn into liquid water that occupies only about three-quarters of the space in each mould.

EXPERIMENTAL ERRORS

ERROR 1 — PRESSURE COOKERS FORCE HEAT INTO FOOD, THEREBY COOKING IT QUICKER

There's a fair bit of nonsense spoken about cooking methods, such as how pressure cookers work. 'Pressure' IS related to force. It is the force per unit area (atmospheric pressure is about 14.5 pounds per square inch, or psi). But pressure cookers don't actually FORCE heat into food in order to cook it more quickly. The truth about this hot topic is very different.

At normal atmospheric pressure, at sea level on Earth, water boils at 100°C. If much more heat is applied it cannot get hotter as it evaporates away into steam. But if the atmospheric pressure is raised considerably, then water's boiling point rises as well and the water can be heated to higher temperatures without vapourizing. Many pressure cookers raise the pressure to 15psi, which causes water to boil at a temperature of 121°C. *Sizzle!* This super-heated water cooks food more quickly than normal boiling does.

ERROR 2: YOU CAN'T FOLD A PIECE OF PAPER IN HALF MORE THAN SEVEN TIMES

Oh yes you can. In 2002, a Californian high school student named Britney Gallivan bought a giant roll of toilet paper. Then, with the help of her parents, she laid it out in a shopping centre. They managed to fold it in half a record-breaking 12 times. Utterly *loo*-dicrous, but true.

ERROR 3: BREAD GOES STALE BECAUSE IT DRIES OUT

At some point in your life you've probably reached into the bread bin and been disappointed at what's inside – five-day-old bread that is hard, stiff and stale. You just can't eat it. But this staleness is not due to the bread drying out. In fact, quite the opposite.

It is because the bread actually ABSORBS moisture from the air. This causes the starch molecules in the bread to turn into crystals, which makes the bread tough, crumbly and stale. Providing it's not too far gone, stale bread can sometimes be revived if it's popped into the oven for a short while. A blast of heat helps to drive out some of the moisture.

CHEMICAL CONFLICTS

DIAMONDS ARE FOR EVER

Diamonds are used in engagement rings as a long-lasting symbol of couples being together for ever. According to the World Diamond Council, about £4.6 billion-worth of diamonds are sold for jewellery every year. You could buy 30,000 luxury sports cars for that same sum and still have money left over for the petrol!

Other than jewellery, diamonds are used in industry to tip many cutting, drilling and grinding tools. This is because diamond is one of the hardest natural substances on Earth. But that doesn't make it indestructible.

Diamonds are cut and polished into gemstones for jewellery, and can be chipped or cracked during the process, or damaged afterwards when worn. These stones are also brittle enough to be shattered with a powerful hammer blow (don't ever try it!) – and, because they are made of carbon, they can also burn in oxygen at temperatures above 720–800°C, or in air at temperatures above 850–1000°C.

ERROR 2 — A LEMON BATTERY WILL POWER A STANDARD TORCH BULB

To all those naughty authors who have included this experiment in their books without actually attempting it first, shame on you! It simply doesn't work and here's why.

A piece of copper (such as a copper coin) and a piece of zinc (such as a galvanized nail) stuck into the acidic juices of a fresh lemon do create a small amount of electricity. If wires from the zinc and copper are attached to a small loudspeaker you would hear a slight crackle of noise. That's electricity calling!

Milliamps (one-thousandths of an ampere) are a measure of electric current. A single lemon battery might generate a current of 1–5 milliamps, while a typical incandescent bulb used in a torch requires between 250 and 500 milliamps to glow brightly. You would therefore need a whole basketful of lemons as batteries to power a humble torch bulb! The way to get this experiment to work is to use a tiny LED (light-emitting diode) used in electronics. LEDs require less electricity to light, but even an LED may still require two or three lemons to power it.

METAL MYTHS

ERROR 1 COPPER IS THE BEST METAL CONDUCTOR OF ELECTRICITY

Copper is a great conductor of electricity. It is used to make millions of metres of electrical wiring every year.

Copper allows electric currents to flow without much loss of energy. Its winding coils are found in electric motors, generators and electromagnets. These feature in all kinds of devices, from loudspeakers to cranes. The average car has about 1,500m of copper wire.

So, copper is a better conductor than gold, tungsten, zinc, iron and most other metals, but it is not the best. The prize for champion conductor goes to silver, which is about seven per cent more conductive than copper. Silver isn't used as widely as copper in electrical wiring, simply because it is more expensive.

Ag (Silver)

Cu (Copper)

ONLY IRON AND STEEL ARE ATTRACTED TO MAGNETS

ERROR 2

False! Other materials containing iron, such as haematite and magnetite, are attracted to magnets, as are the metals nickel and cobalt. Some materials are 'paramagnetic'. This means they are attracted to magnets but only very weakly. Paramagnetic metals include magnesium, molybdenum, lithium and aluminium.

Al (Aluminium)

Li (Lithium)

LEAD PENCILS CONTAIN LEAD

ERROR 3

If you believe this, grab your pencil and write, 'There's no lead in lead pencils' 100 times! The 'lead' in a black lead pencil is not a metal – it is mostly graphite, often mixed with clay. Graphite is a form of carbon, first discovered in England's Lake District during the 16th century. According to legend, shepherds found a deposit of graphite under some trees that had been ripped up during storms. The shepherds called it 'black lead' because this is what it most resembled to them. The name has stuck over the centuries.

Today, pencils are made by grinding graphite finely, mixing it with clay and water, and pressing it together at high temperatures to form thin rods. The result is a writing marvel, able to work upside down and in space. The average pencil can write 45,000 words or draw a line more than 40km long.

TOTALLY INVENTED

ERROR 1 JAMES WATT INVENTED THE STEAM ENGINE

It is not possible for James Watt to have invented the steam engine.

That's because every biography about the great Scottish engineer notes how he first became interested in steam in 1763, when he was asked to repair a model Newcomen steam engine owned by the University of Glasgow. By this time, Newcomen steam engines had been used for 50 years to pump water out of mines. Thomas Newcomen's 1712 invention was actually an improvement of a steam engine built by English inventor Thomas Savery in 1698. Others before him, such as Frenchman Denis Papin, had also dabbled with using steam to drive pistons (solid cylinders that move under pressure).

Watt refined and developed the existing steam engines of his time dramatically. He designed versions that were far more efficient and powerful. His engines generated enough power for the pistons to be able to turn wheels. This paved the way for their use in factories and on tracks as steam trains.

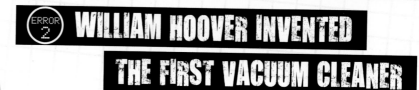

ERROR 2 — WILLIAM HOOVER INVENTED THE FIRST VACUUM CLEANER

In 1907, American inventor James Murray Spangler built a portable suction cleaner powered by electricity. Spangler later sold the rights to his vacuum cleaner to his cousin's husband – a man called William Henry Hoover, who had worked in the leather tanning industry. The Hoover Company went on to become a famous vacuum cleaner manufacturer, but Spangler's invention wasn't the first machine to use air to suck carpets clean. Various inventors had experimented with devices, including British engineer Hubert Cecil Booth who, in 1901, began cleaning carpets using a giant, horse-drawn vacuum cleaner that had to be parked outside the buildings it was to clean!

ERROR 3 — SONY INVENTED THE WALKMAN

Before iPods, chunky portable cassette players were all the rage. They were powered by batteries and came with headphones. In 1979, Japanese electronics company Sony created a portable cassette player. It was known as the Stowaway in the UK, the Soundabout in the USA and the Freestyle in Sweden, but it became known worldwide by its Japanese name, Walkman. In the space of 16 years, Sony made more than 150 million Walkmans. Yet Sony was not the first to build a portable cassette player. Seven years earlier, in Brazil, Andreas Pavel invented the Stereobelt, also powered by batteries and wearable around the hips. In 2003, Sony paid a large sum of money to Pavel, to acknowledge that he was the true pioneer of personal, portable music.

DOUBTING THOMAS

ERROR 1 THOMAS EDISON INVENTED THE ELECTRIC LIGHT BULB

Let's shed some light on this one. Brainy inventor Thomas Edison held more than 1,000 patents (rights to products) for his innovations. Among his inventions were film cameras, batteries, the carbon microphone and even a piano made of concrete!

He is most famous for popularizing incandescent light bulbs — the type of bulb used for at least a century before the arrival of more energy-efficient, compact fluorescent bulbs.

Incandescent bulbs (below) use electricity to heat a thin wire filament until it gets hot enough to glow and give off light. Edison and his team experimented with dozens of different designs before going public in 1879.

His light bulbs proved practical, long-lasting and popular, but they weren't the first. Many people have produced electric light bulbs, starting with British inventor Sir Humphry Davy in 1802. Bulb boffins also included Russian inventor Alexander Lodygin, French magician Jean Eugène Robert-Houdin, and two Canadians, Henry Woodward and Mathew Evans, who sold their 1874 patent to Thomas Edison.

ERROR 3: THOMAS CRAPPER INVENTED THE FLUSHING TOILET

Mr Crapper was a plumber and sanitation engineer who lived in Victorian England. He gained the royal seal of approval in the 1880s when supplying 30 toilets to Edward, Prince of Wales (later King Edward VII). Crapper made improvements to toilets and plumbing, but the first flushing loo was built long before him, all the way back in 1592, by English writer and nobleman Sir John Harrington. He named his toilet Ajax, had it fitted in his home, wrote a book about it and then had a second version installed in Richmond Palace for his godmother – who just happened to be Elizabeth I, Queen of England.

ERROR 2: THOMAS EDISON INVENTED THE FIRST SOUND RECORDING MACHINE

It is true that Thomas Edison invented the phonograph, in 1877, which could record sound waves onto a cylinder covered in tin foil. Although it was the first device to replay sounds, it wasn't the first to record them. Twenty years earlier, French bookseller and printer Édouard-Léon Scott de Martinville patented his phonautograph. This machine converted the vibrations of sound waves into a pattern, etched by a needle, on paper covered in soot from an oil lamp. In 2008, French scientists replayed an 1860 recording made using the phonautograph, converting the lines on paper into the sound of a woman singing.

FAMOUS FABRICATIONS

 ALBERT EINSTEIN FAILED MATHS AT SCHOOL

Hermann and Pauline's son, Albert, was born in 1879 and grew up to become one of the world's greatest scientists. He wrote more than 300 scientific papers and is famous for his energy equation, $E=MC^2$. It could just as well stand for Einstein = Maths Champion.

Far from being a dunce at maths, Albert knew his numbers. At the age of nine, he entered the Luitpold-Gymnasium, a secondary school in Munich, Germany. By the age of 12 he was already studying calculus, a branch of maths that was usually taught only to children of 15 years and older at the school.

Einstein failed to get into the highly rated Federal Polytechnic Academy in Zurich, Switzerland, aged 16 (when every other entrant was 18), but this was due to doing less well in science and non-maths subjects such as French. He passed the entrance exam the following year, and in 1900, aged 21, Einstein qualified as a teacher... of physics and mathematics.

IO

CALLISTO

GANYMEDE

$e=md^2$

$E=MC^2$

$e=cm^2$

EUROPA

ERROR 2 GALILEO INVENTED THE TELESCOPE

Nearly, but not quite. Glass lenses had been made for several centuries by the time enterprising spectacle-makers in the Netherlands placed lenses in tubes to create the first telescopes. These inventions all came at once in 1608: at least three different people – Hans Lippershey, Jacob Metius and Zacharias Janssen – all built and demonstrated early telescopes. Italian astronomer Galileo Galilei learned of these advances just months afterwards and created his own versions with great success. His first 8x magnification telescope wowed Venice in 1609, and in January 1610 he used a telescope with 20x magnification to discover four large moons orbiting around Jupiter.

ERROR 3 MARIE CURIE IS THE ONLY WOMAN TO WIN THE NOBEL PRIZE FOR PHYSICS

I'm very clever

Born in Warsaw, Poland, Marie Curie was a world-renowned scientist who, along with her husband Pierre, discovered the elements polonium and radium, and performed valuable research into radioactivity. In 1903, Marie and Pierre Curie, along with Henri Becquerel, won the Nobel Prize for Physics. This was the first time a female scientist had won the prize, but it was not the only time. Sixty years later, Germany's Maria Goeppert Mayer won the 1963 Nobel Prize for Physics for her investigations into the structure of an atom's nucleus (core). However, Marie Curie is the only woman to have won two Nobel Prizes, with the second prize – for chemistry – being awarded to her in 1911.

SPACE ODDITIES

PLUTO

MYSTERY EXOPLANET

ERROR 1: THERE ARE NINE PLANETS IN THE SOLAR SYSTEM

When the planet Pluto was discovered in 1930, by American astronomer Clyde Tombaugh, every child at school learned that Pluto was the ninth planet in the Solar System. But in 2006, the furthest planet from the Sun got a downgrade.

The International Astronomical Union (IAU) is a group of big boffins who decide on the naming and classifications of things in space. In 2006, they decided that Pluto is not a planet. They said it should be classified as part of a group that includes Ceres (the largest asteroid in the Solar System) and Eris (a 'dwarf planet' that is fractionally bigger than Pluto). Pluto has a smaller diameter than our Moon, and it is now known – like Eris – as a dwarf planet. This is planetary relegation to a lower league!!

ERROR 2 — THE ASTEROID BELT IS A DENSELY PACKED FIELD OF ROCKS

Between Mars and Jupiter lies a giant belt of rocky objects. It contains millions of asteroids, and more than 1.7 million of them are bigger than 1km in diameter. It sounds like a crowded place, but in fact the belt mainly consists of empty space: only about 250 of the asteroids have a diameter of 100km or more. The belt is also vast – it is more than 300 million km wide, so the asteroids are really spaced out, man!

JUPITER

ERROR 3 — JUPITER IS THE MOST MASSIVE PLANET WE KNOW ABOUT

With a diameter of 142,984km, there is no question that Jupiter is the biggest planet in our Solar System. To give you an idea of its size, lump all the other Solar System planets together and you still only get 40 per cent of Jupiter's mass. But Jupiter is neither the biggest nor the most massive planet that exists. Advances in astronomy have allowed us to explore the Universe in greater detail, and in the 1990s astronomers began to discover exoplanets – planets that lie outside of our Solar System. So far, as many as 55 exoplanets have been found to be larger than Jupiter. An object called Kappa Andromedae b, located about 170 light years from Earth, could be one of the largest exoplanets ever found. It has roughly 13 times more mass than Jupiter. What a whopper! Astronomers are checking to see if it really is a planet.

LUNAR LUNACY

 ERROR 1

THERE IS NO GRAVITY ON THE MOON

Wrong, wrong, WRONG! There is plenty of gravity on the Moon, but less than there is on Earth... about five-sixths or, to be more accurate and scientific, 83.3 per cent less.

This reduced gravity means that you would be able to jump up to six times higher on the Moon than you can on Earth. And if you weighed about 30kg on Earth, then you would weigh only 4.9kg on the Moon. Gravity is the force of attraction, and the more massive an object (the more mass or stuff it contains), the greater its force of gravity. The Earth has a diameter of about 12,742km, while the Moon's diameter is about 3,474km. As a result, the Moon's gravity is weaker – but it still has a fair bit of it. Otherwise, those daring astronauts who landed on the Moon wouldn't have been able to walk on its surface. They, along with all their kit, including three lunar roving vehicles, would have just floated away.

ERROR 2

THE MOON IS NEARER TO US WHEN IT IS ON THE HORIZON

This is known as the 'Moon Illusion', and it's just your brain playing tricks on you. When the Moon rises, your eyes see it in the distance next to mountains or big buildings. Your brain knows that these distant objects would appear very large if you were closer to them. This psychological effect is transferred to the Moon, which your brain now thinks is bigger and nearer than it actually is.

ERROR 3 — THERE'S A DARK SIDE OF THE MOON

The Moon completes one full turn about its axis (the invisible line that runs from its north pole to its south pole) every time it completes an orbit around our planet. This means that it always presents the same side of its surface to Earth, so we always see the same part of the Moon, called the near side. The far side of the Moon cannot be seen from Earth, but that doesn't make it dark. Space probes have seen the far side, as have astronauts orbiting the Moon, and it was definitely not permanently dark. Just like Earth, it is lit up for periods of time by light from the Sun.

BY A DISTANCE OF ABOUT 3.8CM EVERY YEAR.

LOST IN SPACE

THE FIRST SPACECRAFT ON THE MOON WAS AMERICAN

You may know that the first people on the Moon were Americans Neil Armstrong and Edwin 'Buzz' Aldrin, who stepped onto the lunar surface in 1969.

However, their *Apollo 11* spacecraft was not the first spacecraft on the Moon. Ten years earlier, the *Luna 2* space probe, built by the Soviet Union, deliberately crashed into the Moon. Another Soviet craft, called *Luna 9*, made the first ever successful 'soft landing' on the Moon in 1966.

TO THE MOON

THE USA SPENT MILLIONS ON A PEN THAT WROTE IN SPACE

This story is not quite write, sorry, right. Regular pens rely on gravity for the ink to flow, so they are no good in space. Both American and Soviet astronauts used pencils in space at first, but bits of lead can break off and float around, so they aren't ideal. In the 1960s, the Fisher Pen Company developed their ingenious AG-7 anti-gravity pen, which used a special ink and pressurized cartridges. These pens could write in space, upside down and even underwater. NASA started using Fisher's space pens on spaceflights from 1967 onwards, but didn't pay millions for the privilege. According to the Associated Press news agency, NASA paid just $2.39 (£1.50) per pen when they made a bulk order in 1968 – the same price the Soviet Union paid a year later when ordering 100 space pens.

THE *APOLLO 11* LUNAR MODULE HAD NO OUTSIDE DOOR HANDLE, SO ASTRONAUTS NEIL ARMSTRONG

VELCRO® AND TEFLON® WERE DEVELOPED BY THE U.S. SPACE PROGRAMME

ERROR 3

Freeze-dried foods, cordless power tools, scratch-resistant spectacle lenses and many advanced materials were the results of research conducted in and around America's space programme. But Velcro®, which was used on astronauts' spacesuits, was definitely not one of them. Velcro®'s series of microscopic hooks and loops was inspired by the hook-like burrs of the burdoch plant that George de Mestral found sticking to his clothes and his dog's fur. The Swiss engineer patented his invention in 1955 and millions of metres of Velcro® are now produced every year.

Teflon® was discovered a decade before Velcro®, in 1938, by American chemist Dr Roy Plunkett. Technically called polytetrafluoroethylene, or PTFE for short, Teflon® is used to create non-stick pots and pans, low-friction parts in many machines, and as a coating for rocket nose cones.

WEATHER OR NOT

ERROR 1 YOUR HOME CAN SURVIVE A TORNADO IF YOU OPEN ALL THE WINDOWS

Tornadoes are fast-spinning columns of air reaching down to the ground from the base of a thunderstorm. The fastest and nastiest can generate wind speeds of up to 480km/h. However, many myths about tornadoes need to be blown away.

For example, it is claimed that tornadoes cannot occur in winter, but this is false. The USA experiences an average of 22 tornadoes every January. It is said that tornadoes cannot take place in big cities, yet tornadoes have struck Dallas, Miami and St Louis among other major metropolises. Another myth is that opening windows in a house can help to save it from tornado destruction.

It has been suggested that this would allow the fast-moving air to move through the house and out the other side, rather than building up enormous pressures on the outside and crushing it. Again, this is untrue. The erratically moving air can still cause enormous damage, and carries with it deadly debris, such as rocks and cars, which crash through buildings whether the windows are open or not.

SUMMER OCCURS WHEN THE EARTH'S ORBIT BRINGS IT CLOSER TO THE SUN

It sounds feasible. After all, Neptune (far from the Sun) is cold, Mercury (close to the Sun) is hot, and Earth's oval orbit does bring it closer and further away from the Sun at different times. But the point at which Earth is furthest from the Sun is in July – the height of summer for people in the northern hemisphere (top half) of the planet.

So how do summer and winter work? It's all down to Earth being tilted by an angle of 23.44°. As one hemisphere of the planet is tilted towards the Sun, the rays strike it more directly and it experiences warmer temperatures and more hours of daylight – summer in other words. At the same time, the other half experiences the opposite – winter. This situation is reversed six months later.

LIGHTNING NEVER STRIKES TWICE IN THE SAME PLACE

Oh yes it does! That's why some tall buildings in stormy areas are often fitted with lightning conductors. These conductive rods channel the electrical power of a major lightning storm away from buildings and safely into the ground, to help prevent structural damage. According to the US National Weather Service Forecast Centre, the Empire State Building in New York City is struck by lightning an average of 23 times per year.

ALL OVER THE PLACE

ERROR 1 ICEBERGS ARE MADE OF FROZEN OCEAN WATER

These huge pieces of ice break off from glaciers or giant ice sheets, such as those found covering Antarctica and large parts of Greenland.

The process of breaking away is called calving, which leaves the icebergs floating in the sea. This is the key to proving they're not made from ocean water, which contains dissolved salts. Icebergs float because they consist of ice made of fresh water, which has a lower density than salty seawater. This means the ice can float in the ocean, although most of an iceberg remains under the water.

ERROR 2 — MAUNA LOA IS THE BIGGEST KNOWN VOLCANO

Rising to a lofty 4,170m above sea level in the Pacific Ocean, Mauna Loa makes up half of the island of Hawaii. It is enormous. Yet, move away from Earth and you'll find an even bigger example. Olympus Mons on Mars is truly gigantic. It is a shield volcano with a diameter of 624km and, according to NASA, it stands 25km high, more than two-and-a-half times the height of Mount Everest.

ERROR 3 — WATER SWIRLS DIFFERENTLY IN THE SINK IN THE NORTHERN HEMISPHERE TO HOW IT DOES IN THE SOUTHERN HEMISPHERE

Let's talk about the Coriolis Effect. As the Earth turns around on its axis, it slightly deflects winds to the right in the northern hemisphere (north of the Equator), and to the left in the southern hemisphere (south of the Equator). However, the Coriolis Effect only has a visible effect on large objects travelling over long distances — for example, cloud formations moving for extended periods of time. A sink or bath full of water is not a large enough amount for this effect to really make a difference. The curved shape of the sink or bath, the running current of the water and the shape of the plughole are far more likely to influence the clockwise or anti-clockwise motion of the water as it drains away.

WATERY WRANGLES

ERROR 1 THE DEAD SEA IS THE SALTIEST LAKE IN THE WORLD

The Dead Sea, around 100km east of the Mediterranean Sea, is a remarkable place. At 433m below sea level, its shores are the lowest land on Earth, while people can float with ease in its waters.

This body of water is located in a hot, dry climate, and it has no major outlet for water to come and go. As a result, water evaporates from the lake very quickly, leaving behind large quantities of salts. So yes, the Dead Sea IS seriously salty – it has about 337 grams of salt per litre of water. Regular seawater is more like 31–38g per litre. However, the Dead Sea isn't the world's saltiest body of water. Lake Assal in the African nation of Djibouti is fractionally saltier, with about 348g of salt per litre. Down in Antarctica, Lake Don Juan (more a pond than a lake at 300m long and 100m wide) boasts more than 400g of salt per litre. This high salt content makes it the only lake in Antarctica that never freezes over, even when temperatures drop to −30°C or lower.

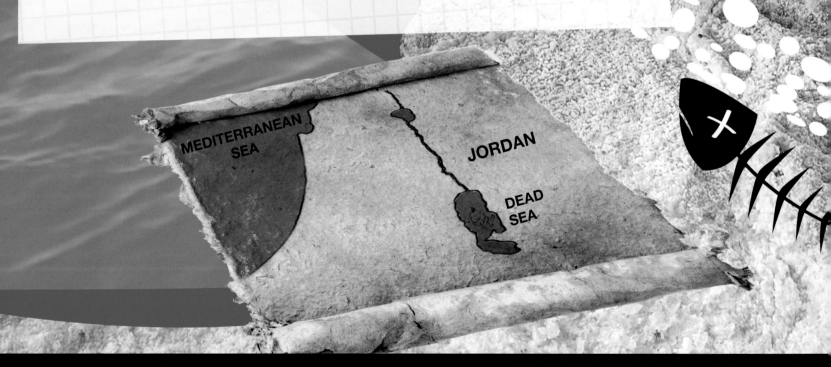

MEDITERRANEAN SEA

JORDAN

DEAD SEA

ERROR 2 — NOTHING LIVES IN THE DEAD SEA

The high levels of salts in the water do make it hard for life to flourish, but the Dead Sea isn't totally lifeless. Small numbers of microscopic bacteria live in the lake, as do *Dunaliella*, which are a type of microscopic algae. In 2011, researchers diving in the Dead Sea also found tiny, single-celled living things called prokaryotes inhabiting small, freshwater springs in the lake bed.

ERROR 3 — ALL RIVERS FLOW FROM NORTH TO SOUTH

Some rivers of the world, such as the Mississippi in the USA and the Mekong in Asia, do flow north to south. But river flow is determined by the local region's geography and gravity. Rivers progress from areas of high land down towards sea level, so they can actually flow in all compass directions. The Rhine flows more than 1,200km northwards through Europe, from the Swiss Alps to the North Sea, while the Nile flows northwards from Central Africa through Sudan and Egypt before emptying into the Mediterranean Sea. It's not just about north or south, either. The Danube in Europe and the Yangtze in China flow west to east, while the Narmada River in India and South Africa's longest river, the Orange, flow east to west.

BUT IT ONCE FLOWED IN THE OPPOSITE DIRECTION!

TRAVEL CHAOS

ERROR 1 CONCORDE WAS THE FIRST SUPERSONIC AIRLINER TO FLY

Supersonic aircraft can fly faster than the speed of sound. Built by France and the UK, *Concorde* was the first supersonic airliner to carry passengers on regular flights, which began in January 1976. But it wasn't the first supersonic airliner to fly.

In 1968, the Soviet Union's Tupolev Tu-144 made its first test flight, more than two months before *Concorde* first flew. The Tu-144 could hold 25 per cent more passengers than *Concorde*, but its development faced problems and it didn't enter service with an airline until November 1977. These flights stopped less than a year later, but the Tu-144s were used to train Soviet astronauts in the 1980s.

ERROR 2 THE JAPANESE BULLET TRAIN IS THE WORLD'S FASTEST RAIL VEHICLE

The first and most famous high-speed train service, Japan's Shinkansen electric train propels about 150 million passengers every year at top speeds of between 240 and 300km/h. The French TGV POS and German ICE 3 trains, though, pip the Shinkansen with speeds of 320km/h, as did China's 350km/h high-speed service between Wuhan and Guangzhou – until its speed was cut to 300km/h in 2011. For the ultimate in fast-tracking, get on board China's Shanghai Maglev Train, which can reach a top speed of 431km/h.

ERROR 3 PLANES DUMP THEIR TOILET WASTE WHILE AIRBORNE

Apart from being illegal, many airliners would endanger themselves if they opened up their bodies in mid-flight to release an unwanted cargo of toilet waste. The differences in air pressure inside the aircraft and outside it, at high altitude, could rip the plane apart. Instead, airliners suck the waste down into holding tanks, which are emptied once the plane is back on the ground. But, very occasionally, accidents do happen. 'Blue ice' is the name given to the mixture of toilet waste and blue-coloured disinfectant that can leak from a plane, freeze on the outside and drop to the ground. *Eurgh!*

ERROR 4 FORMULA ONE CARS ARE THE FASTEST RACING CARS IN THE WORLD

F1 cars are high-performance racing vehicles, with top speeds in the region of 350km/h. They are capable of hitting 0–160km/h and braking back down to zero in less than five seconds. But Top Fuel dragsters are much, much faster. Powered by monster engines running an explosive fuel mixture, these vehicles race along a short, straight drag strip. They get up to 160km/h in as little as 0.7 seconds, and once they've travelled just 200m they are already moving at speeds of 450km/h! The fastest-ever dragster, driven by American Tony Schumacher in 2005, reached 540km/h. Seriously speedy!

WORLD-WIDE WRONGS

ERROR 1 ## GOOGLE WAS THE WORLD'S FIRST INTERNET SEARCH ENGINE

Google is the most famous Internet search engine in the world.

Every day, almost a billion people use it to search for information on the World Wide Web. Google was first developed in 1996–98, but there was already a variety of search engines around. These included Ask AltaVista, Magellan and Excite, which all launched in 1995, as well as Lycos (launched in 1994). And four years earlier, in 1990, three computer science students from Montreal's McGill University, in Canada, produced an Internet search engine called Archie.

ERROR 2 ## WIKIPEDIA IS THE WORLD'S BIGGEST ONLINE ENCYCLOPEDIA

Wikipedia began in 2001. The English language version of the popular online encyclopedia now contains more than 3.9 million entries, from AAA (the American Ambulance Association) to zZz – a Dutch rock band. It sounds impressive, but it's not as big as Baidu Baike. By March 2012, this Chinese online encyclopedia boasted more than 4.6 million entries.

ERROR 3 TIM BERNERS-LEE INVENTED HYPERLINKS

Devisor of the World Wide Web, British researcher Tim Berners-Lee worked at an advanced physics research centre on the border of France and Switzerland. He and a colleague, Belgian Robert Cailliau, put the first web server computer and the first website on the Internet in 1991. The Web uses 'hyperlinks' to navigate between different pages and sites on the Internet. However, hyperlinks were invented not by Tim Berners-Lee but by American Ted Nelson, while he worked on his computer network, called Xanadu, in the early 1960s. In 1968, Douglas Engelbart and his team at Stanford University in California, USA, gave the first public demonstration of hyperlinks in action for a presentation on future computer technology.

ERROR 4 THE FIRST MP3 PLAYER WAS THE IPOD

Apple's first generation iPod was released in November 2001. This was more than three years after the launch of the MPMan F10 – the first MP3 player to go on sale. Built by Saehan Information Systems of South Korea, the F10 contained a small LCD screen and 32 megabytes of flash memory, which was enough to store an album of songs. Diamond, Creative, Archos and Cowon all produced their own MP3 players in the years before the iPod.

While we're at it, the iPad that Apple released in 2010 was certainly not the first tablet computer. The RAND tablet was produced back in 1964 and the Dynabook in 1968. Apple made their own Newton tablets in the early 1990s, and a whole bunch of tablet computers – running Microsoft Windows Tablet Edition – emerged from 2002 onwards.

A NEUTRON STAR IS MADE OF MATTER SQUEEZED INCREDIBLY TIGHTLY TOGETHER. IT IS SO DENSE THAT A TEASPOON OF MATERIAL FROM A NEUTRON STAR WOULD WEIGH MORE THAN 100 MILLION TONNES ON EARTH.

THE HEIGHT OF THE EIFFEL TOWER IN PARIS, FRANCE, VARIES BY UP TO 15CM. THIS IS BECAUSE CHANGES IN TEMPERATURE CAUSE ITS METAL STRUCTURE TO EXPAND OR CONTRACT.

THE IGUAZA FALLS ARE WATERFALLS ON THE BORDER BETWEEN BRAZIL AND ARGENTINA IN SOUTH AMERICA. AT TIMES, MORE THAN 1.3 MILLION LITRES OF WATER FLOW OVER THE FALLS EVERY SECOND.

SCIENTISTS HAVE BUILT A 'NANO-GUITAR', ROUGHLY THE SIZE OF A SINGLE RED BLOOD CELL, WITH STRINGS MEASURING ONLY 100 ATOMS ACROSS. THE GUITAR CAN BE PLAYED USING THE LASERS OF A POWERFUL ATOMIC FORCE MICROSCOPE.

ASTRONAUTS TAKING SPACEWALKS OUTSIDE THEIR SPACECRAFT WEAR SPECIAL LIQUID-COOLED UNDERWEAR, WHICH CONTAINS MORE THAN 80M OF PLASTIC PIPING. COOLED LIQUID RUNS THROUGH THE PIPING, TAKING HEAT AWAY FROM THE BODY.

MARC CHAVANNES AND ALFRED FIELDING INVENTED BUBBLE WRAP, BUT FIRST SOLD IT AS A NOVELTY SHOWER CURTAIN. IT WAS ONLY LATER USED TO PACKAGE FRAGILE GOODS.

A FORMULA ONE CAR IS TYPICALLY MADE OF 80,000 PARTS. THE MONACO GRAND PRIX RACE TAKES PLACE ON ORDINARY ROADS, SO THE MANHOLE COVERS MUST BE WELDED DOWN. THIS IS BECAUSE THE CARS' MOTION CREATES ENOUGH SUCTION TO RIP THEM OUT OF THE GROUND.

RIDICULOUS! BUT TRUE...

HISTORIC HOWLERS

CHAPTER 4

History is packed full of mysteries. Many ancient cultures and civilizations didn't leave behind a written record of how they lived. Archaeologists and historians have to interpret old artefacts to try to work out what happened in history. New discoveries can alter our view of the past.

Even when written records are kept, the details are sometimes shrouded in secrecy or told only from one side — usually that of the winners of battles and the conquerors of foreign lands. Myths frequently glorify rulers and military generals inaccurately. Without both sides of the story, it is hard for historians to build up a true picture of the past.

Some historical myths continue. Turn the page to see false facts about Spartans and Vikings put to the sword, Wild West myths gunned down and dud data on the dead of ancient Egypt laid to rest.

AGE-OLDE ERRORES

ERROR 1 — JUST 300 SPARTANS DEFENDED THERMOPYLAE AGAINST THE PERSIANS

It's a great historical story of how a narrow pass was defended for three days — from a mighty Persian army of more than 100,000 — by just 300 from the Greek city-state of Sparta.

The event has been retold in books, comics and films. Yet, like so many tales from ancient history, a few facts have gone missing in the centuries since.

The narrow pass at Thermopylae was the scene of a battle in 480BCE, as 300 soldiers from Sparta stood firm against the giant Persian army of King Xerxes I. But the 300 Spartans were joined by others from Greek regions, including 400 from Thebes, about 700 from Thespiae and 1,000 from Phocis. All told, the Greek defenders numbered between 4,300 and 8,000 — still a much smaller force than their enemy, but not quite the tiny number that is often stated.

ERROR 2 — SPICES WERE USED IN THE MIDDLE AGES TO DISGUISE THE TASTE AND SMELL OF ROTTEN MEAT

Rotten meat is not only potentially harmful, but it smells rancid and tastes just as bad. Not even a wheelbarrow-load of spices – such as pepper, ginger, cinnamon or cloves – could improve it. In medieval Europe, people tried to eat their meat fresh or they preserved it by drying, smoking, salting or pickling it in brine (salted water).

Spices were grown in Africa and Asia, and had to be carried long distances to Europe.

This was an expensive business. Until the late 15th century, this trade was mostly controlled by the Republic of Venice, which therefore grew rich. In England, during the 1430s, even the most common spice, pepper, was pricey – 500 grams of pepper could cost more than a whole pig! Spices cost much more than buying fresh meat. They were mostly used by the wealthy for new taste sensations, but not to disguise some putrid pork or bad beef.

ERROR 3 — BIOLOGICAL AND CHEMICAL WEAPONS WERE FIRST USED IN WORLD WAR I

Explosives filled with chlorine gas and experiments with anthrax spores during World War I (1914–18) are often claimed to be the first examples of biological and chemical weapons. But using chemicals or disease-spreading living things to harm an enemy has a far longer history. Solon of Athens is said to have used poisonous hellebore plant roots to poison the water supply of the town of Cirrha more than 2,600 years ago. Later, in 1346, the Mongol army laid siege to Caffa (now Feodosiya in the Ukraine) and catapulted dead bodies – infected with plague – over the city walls, hoping to spread the disease among their opponents.

ANCIENT ARGUMENTS

ERROR 1 THE FIRST MUMMIES WERE MADE BY THE ANCIENT EGYPTIANS

Think mummies, think ancient Egypt. We know that this amazing civilization was making mummies at least 5,400 years ago because that is the age of the oldest Egyptian mummy, nicknamed 'Ginger'. But Ginger isn't the oldest known mummy.

You have to scoot over to South America and the hot, dry desert of Atacama in Chile to discover the very oldest. In this region, the Chinchorro culture mummified their dead. They took the bodies apart, treated and preserved them, and then put them back together. Of more than 280 Chinchorro mummies discovered so far, the oldest is a child whose insides had been replaced by vegetable fibres, fur and hair. This mummy is at least 7,000 years old.

ERROR 2 — THE ROMANS HAD ROOMS WHERE THEY COULD THROW UP DURING FEASTS

It's true that wealthy Romans loved a good feed and would think nothing of spending hours at a banquet, gobbling up dish after dish. Exotic foods as wild as stuffed, baked dormouse, flamingo tongue, peacock brain and even elephant's trunk were on the menu. Urgh! But there were no 'vomitoria' (special rooms for them to go and be sick in). Vomitoria did exist in ancient Roman times, but they weren't sick rooms. They were passageways found in stadiums or amphitheatres behind rows of seats, designed to let spectators in and out of the building.

ERROR 3 — EMPEROR NERO PLAYED THE VIOLIN WHILE ROME BURNED

In 64CE, historians believe that a mighty fire devastated parts of the city of Rome. But did the Roman leader of the time, Nero, really just sit back and let it all happen? Accounts by famous Roman writers, such as Tacitus, state that Nero was in his villa in Antium, about 48km from Rome, and rushed to the city when news of the fire reached him. As for playing the violin, Nero didn't even have one. He played the lyre — a small, harp-like instrument with strings that were plucked. The violin as we know it was not invented until about 1,500 years after his death.

WHEN THEIR PET CAT DIED, TO SHOW THEIR GRIEF.

MYSTERIES OF ANCIENT EGYPT

ERROR 1 — TUTANKHAMUN'S TOMB IS CURSED

The lavishly decorated tomb of the young Egyptian pharaoh Tutankhamun was discovered in 1922 by English archaeologist Howard Carter. The following year, as excavations were well underway, the expedition's sponsor, Lord Carnarvon, suddenly died in Cairo.

In the same year, Lord Carnarvon's half-brother died and an American visitor to the tomb, George Jay Gould, also perished. Newspapers suddenly became full of stories of the pharaoh's curse wreaking revenge on anyone who had the nerve to enter the boy-king's tomb of treasures.

Yet amid all this mummy-mania, a few facts were forgotten. Lord Carnarvon suffered blood poisoning from an infected mosquito bite, his half-brother (who had actually never visited Tut's tomb) died in London after a dental operation went wrong, and Gould died of pneumonia in France. The leader of the Tutankhamun expedition, Howard Carter, lived for a further 16 years until 1939. The only journalist allowed at the tomb's discovery was Henry Morton, who passed away at the ripe old age of 86 in 1979. That should wrap things up.

ERROR 3 CLEOPATRA WAS AN ANCIENT EGYPTIAN

Not strictly true. Cleopatra was the daughter of Ptolemy XII (117–51BCE). He could trace his heritage directly back to one of Alexander the Great's generals, named Ptolemy, who came from Macedonia – an ancient kingdom based in what is now northern Greece. Cleopatra was born in 69BCE and, from 51BCE until 30BCE, she ruled Egypt with either her brothers or her son before it became part of the ancient Roman empire.

ERROR 2 CLEOPATRA'S NEEDLE IS A TRIBUTE TO THE PHARAOH QUEEN

There are actually three Cleopatra's Needles around the world – one in New York, one in Paris and a third in London. None of these tall columns, called obelisks, have any connection to the famous Cleopatra who ruled Egypt more than 2,000 years ago. The London and New York obelisks were built during the reign of Pharaoh Thutmose III, who ruled Egypt until his death in 1425BCE. The obelisk in Paris is believed to have been constructed during the reign of Ramesses II, who died in 1213BCE. The famous female queen of Egypt, Cleopatra (Cleopatra VII Philopator), was not born until more than 1,000 years later, in about 69BCE.

INCLUDING SIX CHARIOTS AND MORE THAN 40 PAIRS OF SANDALS.

MONUMENTAL MISTAKES

ERROR 1 — THE GIANT PYRAMIDS OF ANCIENT EGYPT WERE BUILT BY SLAVES

The Great Pyramid and other pyramids found in ancient Egypt are no longer thought to have been built by thousands of captured slaves. New archaeological finds, including the tombs of pyramid workers buried near pyramids, have altered that view.

Egyptologists now believe that many of those who built some of the ancient world's biggest pyramids were farmers and peasants. They worked on these great constructions when there was little work required in the fields, such as when the River Nile flooded its banks and farm fields nearby. In return, the pyramid workers did not have to pay taxes and were provided with food and shelter.

ERROR 2 — THE DRUIDS BUILT STONEHENGE

The Druids were important religious figures in Iron-Age Britain, which began in about 800BCE. The ancient Druids did occasionally use the giant stone circle of Stonehenge for worship, but they certainly didn't build it. Radiocarbon dating techniques have found that Stonehenge was built in three phases – the earliest beginning in about 3100BCE and the last completed in about 1500BCE, some time before we think the Druids arrived.

PYRAMIDS OF EGYPT

STONEHENGE

ERROR 3 — THERE IS ONLY ONE STATUE OF LIBERTY

New York City's Statue of Liberty is an internationally recognized landmark. It was given to the USA by the people of France and erected in New York City Harbour in 1886. But there is also a 10.5-m-high replica, fashioned in bronze, which is about a quarter of the NYC statue's size. It sits on an island in the River Seine, which flows through Paris, the capital of France. The replica was a gift from Americans living in Paris in 1889.

STATUE OF LIBERTY

ERROR 4 — TOWER BRIDGE IS THE OLDEST BRIDGE IN LONDON

This London icon may look mighty old as it stands close to the Tower of London (begun in the early 1080s), but the nearby bridge is a baby, completed in 1894. Blackfriars Bridge (1869), Battersea Railway Bridge (1863), Westminster Bridge (1862) and Grosvenor Bridge (1859) were all constructed earlier. Further west, Richmond Bridge is even older, built in 1777. Historians believe that the first bridge over the River Thames in London was built by the Romans in 50CE. London Bridge, as it was called, has been replaced four times – the latest one dates from 1973.

TOWER BRIDGE

OLYMPIC OVERSIGHTS

ERROR 1 — THE ANCIENT OLYMPICS WERE THE WORLD'S FIRST MULTI-SPORT EVENT

Held at Olympia in Greece from 776BCE onwards, the Greek Olympics grew into a major event in the ancient world, but they were not the first games held.

The Tailteann Games in Ireland may have been held as early as 1829BCE. They featured running, spear and stone throwing, as well as jumping and wrestling competitions. The ancient Egyptians, who engaged in many sports including gymnastics, high jumping, swimming and early forms of hockey and boxing, may have also held their own sports events long before the Greeks. An image, more than 4,600 years old, shows the Egyptian pharaoh Djoser taking part in a running race during a festival.

IN THE ANCIENT SPORT OF PANKRATION (A MIXTURE OF BOXING AND WRESTLING),

ERROR 2 · THE FIRST OLYMPIC CHEATS WERE THOSE WHO USED DRUGS

Canadian sprinter Ben Johnson, who was disqualified at the 1988 Olympics, is one of a number of Olympians who have used banned drugs to improve their performance. But these athletes were not the first to cheat at the games. Back in 1904, American marathon runner Fred Lorz won the race looking surprisingly fresh – due to the fact he had hitched a lift in a car for 17.7km of the 42.2-km race. The rotter!

Athletes at the ancient Olympics made a promise to follow the rules by placing their hands on slices of raw boar flesh in front of a giant statue of Zeus. It didn't stop a few cheating. These included boxer Eupolus who bribed three of his opponents at the 338BCE games to let him win. They were all heavily fined. A century earlier, when Sparta was banned from competing, Lichas from Sparta entered his chariot horses in a race pretending to be from Thebes. He was caught and flogged.

ERROR 3 · ALL OLYMPIC WINNERS RECEIVED MEDALS MADE OF GOLD

At the ancient Greek Olympics, winners didn't receive medals. Instead, they received a crown of leaves to wear on their head, but were sometimes rewarded by their home regions with free houses, meals or large jars of olive oil. At the first modern Olympics in 1896, winners received silver medals and runners-up were given copper ones. Solid gold medals were awarded at the 1912 Olympics in Stockholm, but since then the medals tend to be mostly silver (at least 92.5 per cent silver these days) and plated in a very thin layer of gold.

SOSTRATOS OF SICYON BROKE HIS OPPONENTS' FINGERS UNTIL THEY GAVE IN.

FIGHTING A LOSING BATTLE

ERROR 1 THE VIKINGS WORE HORNED HELMETS AND DRANK FROM HUMAN SKULLS

No group in history get a worse press than the Norsemen, or Vikings. They were portrayed as barbarous, unruly and violent, but only a small number of all Vikings were warriors. Many were peaceful farmers.

And that's not the only myth about Vikings. The horned helmet is thought to have been invented by writers and artists long after the Vikings existed, with the horns making them look more evil and terrifying. None of the helmets or parts of Viking helmets found by archaeologists has ever featured these horns.

Another Norse no-show were human skulls fashioned into drinking cups. This myth probably came from a history book written in the 1600s by Ole Worm, which described Vikings drinking from the 'curved branches of skulls'. Worm meant cups made from cattle and goat horns, but mistranslations led to these parts of animal skulls being mistaken for the *human* heads of Viking enemies.

PIRATES MADE MAPS OF THEIR BURIED TREASURE

ERROR 2

Another feared group on the high seas were pirates, especially during the 16th, 17th and 18th centuries. Most pirates spent their captured loot as quickly as they got it and very, very few ever buried it. One who did was Sir Francis Drake in 1573, but he only buried the treasure because his crew couldn't carry it all overland in one journey. When they returned, soon afterwards, they discovered it had already been dug up and taken. With little treasure ever buried, there was no need for real-life buried treasure maps. Those seen in books and films are works of fiction.

THE VIKINGS ALWAYS SAILED IN LONGSHIPS

ERROR 3

Vikings famously used long, narrow ships, powered by sails and oars, on their travels and conquests. These longships were fast and nimble, yet they could hold 70–120 people. However, longships were just one type of ship that the Vikings built and sailed. Knarrs were cargo ships, which were shorter but wider than longships. These were used on voyages across the Atlantic to Greenland, and also on trade routes across the Baltic and North seas. Karves were another type of Viking ship, smaller than knarrs. They had a very shallow hull, enabling them to transport people and livestock from sea to shore.

MOST DESIGNS FEATURED SWORDS, TORN HEARTS AND OTHER SYMBOLS.

HOW THE LAND LIES

ERROR 1 — MAGELLAN WAS THE FIRST EXPLORER TO SAIL RIGHT AROUND THE WORLD

In 1519, Portuguese explorer Ferdinand Magellan led a fleet of five ships from Spain to voyage westwards...

Three years later, one of Magellan's five ships, *Victoria*, captained by Spaniard Juan Sebastián Elcano, returned to Spain. This ship had succeeded in crossing the Atlantic, Pacific and Indian oceans on its voyage, but it carried less than ten per cent of the 270 sailors who had set off. Magellan himself was not among them, having been killed during a battle on the island of Mactan in the Philippines. It was the expedition's survivors, led by Elcano, who were the first to sail around the world.

ERROR 2 — CAPTAIN COOK DISCOVERED AUSTRALIA

English Captain James Cook sailed his ship, *HMS Endeavour*, along much of the eastern coast of Australia in 1770, first landing at Botany Bay (now part of the large city of Sydney). Cook returned in triumph, but he wasn't the first to discover the giant landmass. In 1606, Dutch sailor Willem Janszoon landed on Cape York, the northernmost tip of what is now the Australian state of Queensland. Englishman William Dampier, as well as Dutch sailors including Dirk Hartog and Abel Tasman, also reached parts of Australia before Cook made his voyage.

ERROR 3 — HERNANDO CORTÉS WAS THE FIRST EUROPEAN TO VIEW THE PACIFIC OCEAN

In 1513, Spanish explorer Vasco Núñez de Balboa crossed Panama, in Central America, and became the first European to set eyes on the mighty Pacific Ocean. At that time, celebrated Spaniard Hernán (or Hernando) Cortés was still living in Cuba, in the Caribbean, and didn't travel to the Central American mainland – where he later conquered the Aztec empire – until 1519.

ERROR 4 — CHRISTOPHER COLUMBUS DISCOVERED AMERICA

America may have been first 'discovered' by peoples migrating from Asia as early as 40,000 years ago. But, when it comes to Europeans, many think explorer Christopher Columbus got there first. He didn't. In 1492, he crossed the Atlantic to reach the Caribbean region, landing at both the Bahamas and the island of Hispaniola (now Haiti and the Dominican Republic) before returning to Europe. On this and his three other Atlantic voyages, Columbus never reached the coast of what would become the USA. Long before Columbus, 11th-century Viking explorer Leif Erikson may have reached Canada. Also, 11 years after Columbus's first voyage, Spanish explorer Juan Ponce de León landed in what is now the US state of Florida.

AMERICA
EUROPE
THE ROUTES OF COLUMBUS
ATLANTIC OCEAN
AFRICA
CARIBBEAN SEA

AMISS IN AMERICA

 ERROR 1

BETSY ROSS DESIGNED THE CURRENT U.S. FLAG

The official national flag of the USA is recognized worldwide and is the only flag ever to be planted on the Moon. According to legend, Betsy Ross, a seamstress from Philadelphia, sewed the first ever American flag in the 1770s.

There is little evidence for Betsy's claim to fame and, even if it were true, the Stars and Stripes flag has undergone more than 20 makeovers since it was first flown in 1777.

It is easy to prove who designed the flag that flies today. Robert Heft was an Ohio high school student who designed a new version of the Stars and Stripes, with 50 stars (to represent the 50 states), for a homework assignment in 1958. He received a B-minus for his efforts at school, but when his design was eventually adopted by the US Congress and became the flag we see today, his grade was upped to an A!

ERROR 2 — HENRY HUDSON DISCOVERED THE HUDSON RIVER

English explorer Henry Hudson was hired by traders in the 1600s to find a sailing route westwards from Europe to Cathay (China). Hudson crossed the Atlantic and, although he did not find a route, he did sail down what we now call the Hudson river and reached the large bay that is today the site of New York City Harbour. In the process, he found his way to the gigantic Hudson Bay, which is where he perished, in 1611, after a mutiny left him, his son and seven loyal crew members adrift in a small boat. But Hudson was not the first European to observe the Hudson river. That honour goes to Italian explorer Giovanni da Verrazzano, who reached the river's mouth back in 1524.

ERROR 3 — THE U.S. DECLARATION OF INDEPENDENCE WAS SIGNED ON 4TH JULY

In 1776, 13 American colonies agreed to declare their independence from the British empire at a meeting in Philadelphia called the Second Continental Congress. One of them was John Adams (later the second US president) who wrote to his wife that, 'The Second Day of July 1776 will be the most memorable... in the History of America.'

Not quite. The date etched in American history is two days later – 4 July. It took two whole days to produce and edit a document called the Declaration of Independence, which was then sent to the printers. Signing the declaration didn't begin until 2 August 1776. One of the 56 signatures belonged to a representative named Matthew Thornton, from New Hampshire, who did not even sign until November.

(CHARITY SHOP) FOR LESS THAN £2 AND SOLD AT AUCTION IN 2007 FOR MORE THAN £280,000.

BY GEORGE!

ERROR 1 — THE FIRST PRESIDENT OF THE U.S.A. HAD WOODEN TEETH

George Washington was commander-in-chief during the American Revolution of the 18th century, in which American colonies broke away from British rule. In 1789, Washington gained 100 per cent of the vote to become the first President of the USA.

He certainly didn't lack popular support; the only thing he did lack was teeth. He is said to have had only one real tooth remaining by the time he took office as president.

Washington's teeth started falling out in his early twenties and he visited many dentists before settling on Dr John Greenwood, who made him sets of false teeth. None of these sets featured wooden teeth. Instead, Greenwood used a mixture of materials including Washington's own teeth, cows' teeth and carved pieces of tooth from a hippopotamus!

ERROR 2 — AS PRESIDENT, WASHINGTON LIVED IN THE WHITE HOUSE

All presidents since George Washington have made the White House their home, except for the man himself. George helped to choose its site and supervised its construction, but he died before it was completed. The first occupants of the White House were John and Abigail Adams, in 1800.

ERROR 3 · GEORGE WASHINGTON CHOPPED DOWN A CHERRY TREE

After chopping down a cherry tree, six-year-old George Washington admits his crime to his father, saying, "I can't tell a lie, Pa". It's a lovely story illustrating Washington's honesty. The only thing is, it's almost certainly made up. The story appeared in a biography of Washington written shortly after his death. People say that its author, Mason Locke Weems, filled some of the pages about Washington's early life with tall tales that made him look more heroic.

ERROR 4 · GEORGE WASHINGTON THREW A SILVER DOLLAR ACROSS THE POTOMAC RIVER

How far can you throw a coin? If you can hurl it half the length of a football pitch, you've done well. That's a distance of about 50m, but the Potomac river is more than 1,600m wide – so it's simply impossible to chuck a small, metal disc across it! This story is meant to highlight Washington's strength as a young man, but it is a myth for another reason as well. There were no silver dollar coins when Washington was younger. The first were minted in 1794, just five years before his death.

WESTERN WRONGS

ERROR 1 — BUFFALO BILL GOT HIS NAME FROM HUNTING BUFFALO

American cowboy William F Cody, or 'Buffalo Bill' as he was better known, competed in an eight-hour shooting contest with William Comstock for the right to use that nickname in the late 1860s.

Cody won the shoot-out, and later used the nickname in books and publicity for his travelling show throughout North America and Europe.

However, Buffalo Bill never shot a single buffalo in his life. Buffalo do not exist in the wild in the USA. Instead, Cody had been shooting American bison for food. Bison have thicker fur, a large shoulder hump and a far bigger head than buffalos, which are found mostly in Asia and Africa.

WANTED!

ERROR 2 — BILLY THE KID KILLED 21 MEN IN GUNFIGHTS BEFORE HE WAS 21

It makes for easy arithmetic, but feared outlaw Billy the Kid gunned down far fewer victims. Four shootings committed solely by Billy — real name William McCarty Jr and not William Bonney as many think — have been confirmed. Five more shootings occurred as a result of gunfights that Billy's gang were involved in.

ERROR 3 — DODGE CITY AND TOMBSTONE WERE WILD WEST MURDER CAPITALS

The names of these frontier towns were meant to strike fear into the hearts of the more genteel folk who lived far from the Wild West. Gunfights and murders were thought to occur there every day, a fact reinforced ever since by hundreds of television and film westerns. Although the towns were rough and brawls occurred regularly, murders weren't quite as common as people think. Between 1876 and 1885, there were 17 murders in Dodge City. 1878 was the worst year, with five killings. This number matched Tombstone's most murderous year in 1881, when the famous gunfight at the O.K. Corral occurred. In comparison, there were 324 murders in Philadelphia in 2011.

ERROR 4 — WILD WEST GUNFIGHTS WERE QUICK-ON-THE-DRAW DUELS

Few gunfights were honourable duels between two lone gunfighters facing each other, 20 paces apart, in a deserted street. Many shoot-outs were sudden acts of mayhem, often in crowded areas with a number of gunslingers shot in the back. Shots were fired usually at close range from a single gun, because firing two guns at the same time, accurately, is almost impossible.

IN HIS POCKET AND KILLED HIMSELF IN 1893.

WOMEN'S WOES

 ERROR 1

WITCHES WERE BURNED AT THE STAKE IN THE SALEM WITCH TRIALS

This spellbinding fact is really hocus-pocus. In the past, witches were sometimes burned to death, but not those involved in history's most infamous witch trial.

In the village of Salem in the USA, 20 citizens, mostly women, were accused of witchcraft and found guilty in 1692. The fate for 19 of them was hanging, while the last citizen (an 80-year-old man) was crushed under a huge weight of stones placed upon his body. It was a grisly end for all of them, but there wasn't a fire in sight.

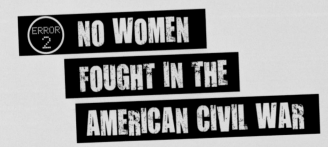

ERROR 2

NO WOMEN FOUGHT IN THE AMERICAN CIVIL WAR

Both the Confederate and Union armies refused to allow women to join up as soldiers. That didn't stop some women from disguising themselves as men in order to fight. Records show that more than two dozen female soldiers were either killed in action, wounded or taken prisoner. Some historians believe that as many as 250 women, and possibly more, saw action. Among them were Sarah Edmonds, who joined the Second Michigan Infantry in 1861 under the false name Franklin Thompson, and Jennie Hodgers, who joined the 95th Illinois Infantry as Albert Cashier. Jennie fought in many battles and wasn't found to be a woman until long after the war ended.

CAPTURED 18TH-CENTURY FEMALE PIRATES ANNE BONNEY AND MARY READ BOTH ESCAPED BEING HANGED

ROMAN GLADIATORS WERE ALL MALE

ERROR 3

Not all! Some were women. A female gladiator was known as a gladiatrix. Gladiators either fought each other or were pitted against armed dwarfs as bloodthirsty Roman entertainment. Historians believe that gladiatrices fought in games during the reign of Roman Emperor Nero, but Emperor Severus banned women from fighting as gladiators in 200CE.

BY REVEALING THEY WERE PREGNANT. BRITISH LAW WOULDN'T EXECUTE A MOTHER-TO-BE.

MILITARY MIX-UPS

ERROR 1 — NAPOLEON BONAPARTE WAS SHORT

Though Napoleon Bonaparte began his military career as a humble second lieutenant, he rose through the ranks to become the most feared military leader in Europe, as well as Emperor of France (1804–15).

Napoleon was often described by his enemies as a short, squat man and his real-life nickname was *Le Petit Caporal* ('The Little Corporal'), but was he really a tiny tyrant? His height was often given as 1.57m, making it fair to say he was short. But as is so often the case in history, some important details have been overlooked. In the French system of measurement at that time, the *pouce*, or inch, was almost 10 per cent longer than the British inch, so Napoleon was really about 1.7m tall. This was a typical height for men of Napoleon's era.

ERROR 2 — THE HUNDRED YEARS' WAR LASTED FOR 100 YEARS

You'd think so, wouldn't you? But the truth is more confusing. The Hundred Years' War was actually a series of wars, battles and struggles for control of the throne of France, between French and British kings and their armies. It actually began in 1337 and ended in 1453 – making 116 years in total.

1451

1400

1354

1389

ERROR 3 — LORD NELSON WORE AN EYEPATCH

Famed sailor Horatio Nelson led the British navy to a series of major victories, such as at the Battle of the Nile and the Battle of Trafalgar, where he lost his own life. A large statue of him stands on top of a column in London's Trafalgar Square in the UK. Close examination of the statue doesn't reveal an eyepatch because Lord Nelson didn't actually wear one.

In 1801, during an attack on land at Calvi, in Corsica, a stray bullet caused debris to strike Nelson's right eye. The eye remained in its socket and looked normal, so Nelson chose not to wear a patch – but he could no longer see with it. Paintings of Nelson created during his lifetime never show him sporting an eyepatch. It was many decades after his death that a patch became a feature of his portraits. Even in the 20th century, celebrated actor Laurence Olivier wore a patch while playing the role of Nelson.

FALSE ECONOMIES

ERROR 1 BRITAIN HAS THE OLDEST PARLIAMENT IN THE WORLD

When William of Normandy conquered England in 1066, he put in place a system whereby the king would parlay (talk) and consult with leading nobles and church figures.

In the 13th century, this grew into an organized parliament in which laws and actions were debated by people selected from all over the country. The English (now UK) Parliament is sometimes thought of as the first, but others are older. The parliament of the Isle of Man, called the Tynwald, claims to be the oldest continuous parliament, stretching back more than 1,000 years, while the Kingdom of León in northwestern Spain held a parliament in 1188CE. The Althing (meaning 'assembly') in Iceland is believed to be even older. It was founded in 930CE at Þingvellir and continued to be held there until 1799. In 1844, after a gap of 44 years, it was restored and moved to Reykjavik, Iceland's capital city.

ERROR 2 INDIRA GANDHI WAS THE FIRST WOMAN TO BE VOTED LEADER OF A COUNTRY

In 1966, Indira Gandhi became India's first ever female prime minister. But she was not the first female head of government in the modern world. That honour goes to Sirimavo Ratwatte Dias Bandaranaike who, in 1960, was elected prime minister of Ceylon (now Sri Lanka). Bandaranaike also served as Sri Lankan prime minister in 1970–77 and in 1994–2000.

IN THE 1920s, GERMANY HAD THE HIGHEST INFLATION RATE OF ALL TIME

Inflation is a general rise in the prices of goods and services in a country. You may see politicians on television discussing inflation rates of four, six or eight per cent per year. Hyperinflation, though, is inflation gone mad! During the early 1920s, problems with Germany's economy saw prices go off the scale. In October 1923, the monthly inflation rate reached 29,500 per cent! That meant prices doubled every 3.7 days, and led to people pushing wheelbarrows full of money just to pay for food. Bonkers!

Astonishingly, this wasn't the highest ever rate of inflation. In January 1994, inflation in Yugoslavia reached 313,000,000 per cent with prices doubling every 1.4 days. But there's an even worse example. In early 1946, Hungary's currency (the pengö) collapsed and prices started doubling every 15.5 hours. It was hard to keep up! In 1944, the largest banknote was a 1,000 pengö bill. But by mid-1946, 100,000,000,000,000,000,000 pengö banknotes were being printed. *Ker-ching!*

INDUSTRIAL ACCIDENTS

ERROR 1 HENRY FORD'S FAMOUS 'MODEL T' FORD ONLY CAME IN BLACK

Motor car-making pioneer Henry T Ford wanted to create a cheap, simple, reliable motor car for those who could not afford the cost of expensive early automobiles.

His answer was the Model T Ford, and it became a runaway bestseller. Between 1914 and the mid-1920s, the car was available only in black. Ford is said to have declared (although no one is certain he actually said it) that his cars were available "in any colour so long as it's black".

Yet, when the Model T Ford first came out in 1909, black was nowhere to be seen. The car was available in grey, red or 'Brewster' green. Those colours, along with blue, were reintroduced towards the end of the Model T's life. The cars stopped being made in 1927, the same year that the 15 millionth Model T rolled off the production line.

GERMAN ENGINE INVENTOR RUDOLF DIESEL DEMONSTRATED HIS

CHARLES LINDBERGH WAS THE FIRST PERSON TO FLY NON-STOP ACROSS THE ATLANTIC

ERROR 2

Don't fly off in a rage, but American pilot Charles Lindbergh wasn't the first, second or even third person to cross the Atlantic Ocean in a single non-stop flight. When he flew from New York City, USA, to Paris, France, in 1927, Lindbergh was actually about the 67th person! In 1919, British aviators John Alcock and Arthur Whitten Brown flew a modified Vickers Vimy World War I bomber across the Atlantic for the first time. Following them were airship flights carrying an estimated further 64 people across the Atlantic, before Lindbergh's epic 33.5-hour flight in his single-engined plane named *Spirit of St Louis*.

GEORGE WASHINGTON CARVER INVENTED PEANUT BUTTER

ERROR 3

Born a slave in 1864, agricultural pioneer George Washington Carver promoted alternative crops to cotton. He developed innovative uses of crops — such as peanuts, soybeans and sweet potatoes — so that poor farming families in the USA could sustain themselves. In his laboratories, he came up with hundreds of new uses for these crops, including postage stamp glue made from sweet potatoes and paints made from soybeans. Carver did produce a creamy peanut butter, but peanuts had already been ground into an oily paste and enjoyed by Central and South American civilizations hundreds of years earlier.

TITANIC UNTRUTHS

ERROR 1 TITANIC'S SINKING WAS THE WORST SHIPPING DISASTER OF ALL TIME

When the luxury cruise liner *Titanic* hit an iceberg and sank in the North Atlantic in 1912, more than two-thirds of the passengers and crew lost their lives.

According to the *Encyclopedia Titanica*, there were approximately 2,223 people on board, and an estimated 1,517 perished. Yet this did not make it the world's worst shipping disaster.

Back in 1948, the Chinese steamship *SS Kiangya* sank after hitting an exploding underwater mine. As many as 2,750 people died. The worst peacetime shipping disaster is thought to be the demise of *MV Doña Paz*, a Philippines passenger ferry that collided with a ship and sank. Only 26 survived from the estimated 3,000–4,400 on board. But the worst disaster of all is believed to be the sinking of German ship *MV Wilhelm Gustloff* in the Baltic Sea in 1945. Packed with civilians and soldiers being evacuated, the death toll is estimated at between 5,300 and 9,400.

S.O.S.

TITANIC WAS THE FIRST SHIP TO SEND AN S.O.S.

ERROR 2

In 1909, *SS Arapahoe* was travelling in the Atlantic Ocean when it sent the first ever real-life emergency S.O.S. distress call. It was made by wireless operator TD Haubner, who was on board when an engine shaft broke in the ship. Amazingly, a few months later Haubner also became the second ever person to *receive* an S.O.S. after picking up a distress call from *SS Iroquois* while sailing on *SS Arapahoe*. By the time *Titanic* signalled S.O.S. in 1912, a number of other ships, including *Merida*, *Niobe* and *Lexington*, had also sent S.O.S. signals.

S.O.S. STANDS FOR 'SAVE OUR SHIPS'

ERROR 3

The Morse code signal – made up of three dots, three dashes and three more dots – is known worldwide as the distress signal, S.O.S. It was introduced by Germany in 1905, and the following year, at the International Radiotelegraphic Conference in Berlin, it was adopted as a world standard. But here's the thing – the three letters do not stand for anything. They don't mean 'Save Our Ship', 'Send Us Support' or 'Save Our Souls'. The conference agreed to S.O.S. because the letters formed a quick and easy Morse code message to send, and just as easy a message to receive and understand.

IN 1789, GEORGE WASHINGTON TOOK OUT A BOOK, CALLED *THE LAW OF NATIONS* BY EMER DE VATTEL, FROM A NEW YORK LIBRARY AND NEVER RETURNED IT. THE OVERDUE BOOK HAS MOUNTED UP MORE THAN £209,000 IN LIBRARY FINES.

GUNMAN 'WILD BILL' HICKOCK WAS SHOT DEAD IN THE BACK WHILE PLAYING CARDS. THE FOUR CARDS HE CLUTCHED AS HE DIED WERE THE ACE OF CLUBS, THE ACE OF SPADES AND A PAIR OF EIGHTS. THIS IS KNOWN TODAY AS A 'DEAD MAN'S HAND'.

MONTENEGRO ENTERED A 1904–05 WAR BETWEEN RUSSIA AND JAPAN ON RUSSIA'S SIDE, BUT WERE NOT ASKED TO SIGN THE EVENTUAL PEACE TREATY. AS A RESULT, MONTENEGRO WAS TECHNICALLY AT WAR WITH JAPAN FOR 111 YEARS UNTIL JAPANESE DEPUTY FOREIGN MINISTER AKIKO YAMANAKA VISITED MONTENEGRO IN 2006 TO DECLARE HOSTILITIES OVER.

THE OLDEST BOOMERANG IN EXISTENCE WAS NOT FOUND IN AUSTRALIA, BUT IN POLAND. ABOUT 23,000 YEARS OLD, THE BOOMERANG WAS MADE OF MAMMOTH TUSK AND WAS DISCOVERED IN A CAVE AT OBLAZOWA ROCK IN 1987.

SAILOR WILLIAM REEVES WAS BORN ON 14 APRIL 1912 ON THE DAY *TITANIC* HIT AN ICEBERG AND SANK. IN 1935, REEVES SPOTTED AN ICEBERG WHILE ON BOARD A SHIP. HE ALERTED THE CREW JUST IN TIME TO AVOID A COLLISION. THE SHIP HE WAS ON WAS CALLED *TITANIAN*. SPOOKY!

SOME ANCIENT EGYPTIANS SLEPT ON PILLOWS MADE OF SOLID STONE.

WORLD WONDERS AND BLUNDERS

CHAPTER 5

When it comes to the world and its global population of more than 7 billion people, there's plenty of room for myth and error. Don't forget humans are a species who for many centuries believed the Earth was flat, not round. Other people thought the Earth was carried through space on the back of a giant turtle! Even in recent times, people's knowledge of other parts of the world was far from complete. This has led to mistakes being made and repeated down the generations.

This chapter covers the general ignorance of geography, the myths about movies and music, the slip-ups on sport and the urban myths that take hold as true stories. So, if you think you know the capital of Australia, Thailand or Nauru, who masterminded the moonwalk move, and who made Mickey Mouse, prepare to be surprised.

FACTS ALL AT SEA!

ERROR 1 — THE CANARY ISLANDS ARE NAMED AFTER CANARY BIRDS

The Canary Islands (*Islas Canarias* in Spanish) lie off the Atlantic coast of north Africa. Some of the islands, such as Tenerife, Lanzarote and Fuerteventura, are popular holiday destinations, but the island group is not named after the Canary bird (*Serinus canaria*). In fact, the small yellow bird is actually named after *them*!

So, from where – or from whom – did the islands get their name? The answer is, almost certainly, from the ancient Romans. They sailed to the islands and named them *Insula Canaria* in Latin, which means the 'Isles of Canines' – canines being the fancy word for dogs. Why? Well, there are two main theories. It could be that large wild dogs were on the island, or perhaps the Roman voyagers mistook monk seals on the beaches for big dogs. Whatever the reason, the name stuck, and the modern coat of arms for the islands features a pair of dogs on either side of a shield.

ERROR 2 — THE WORLD HAS FOUR OCEANS: THE ARCTIC, ATLANTIC, INDIAN AND PACIFIC

ARCTIC OCEAN

PACIFIC OCEAN

ATLANTIC OCEAN

INDIAN OCEAN

SOUTHERN OCEAN

The surface of our planet is 71 per cent water, almost all of which is found in the world's seas and oceans. Traditionally, everyone thinks of four oceans – the Arctic, Atlantic, Indian and Pacific – but in 2000, that all changed.

In that year, the International Hydrographic Organization declared the Southern Ocean as the world's fifth ocean. The Southern Ocean surrounds Antarctica, and the southernmost tips of South America and New Zealand are the nearest other major land masses.

ERROR 3
THE CAPE OF GOOD HOPE IS THE SOUTHERNMOST TIP OF AFRICA

Many famous tales tell of explorers sailing around the Cape of Good Hope on voyages to and from the Indian and Atlantic oceans. The Cape is a southerly part of the South African coast, but it is not the most southerly point in Africa (see map, right).

Walker Bay, Quoin Point and Danger Point are all further south. The most southerly of all is Cape Agulhas, which lies about 150km east-southeast of Cape Town and about 50km further south of the Cape of Good Hope.

ERROR 4
ALL SHIPS' CAPTAINS CAN LEGALLY MARRY COUPLES AT SEA

International maritime law gives captains of boats and ships no special powers to marry couples. Some people do hold their wedding parties on cruise ships, but often head to shore for the legal marriage ceremony or are married by a special registrar or minister on board. However, there are a few exceptions: sea captains in Japan can marry couples who hold Japanese passports, while ships registered in Bermuda or Malta also allow their captains to perform marriage ceremonies.

MAPPING MISTAKES

SAHARA

ANTARCTICA

ERROR 1 THE SAHARA IS THE LARGEST DESERT ON EARTH

Oh no it isn't! As deserts go, the Sahara is enormous, yes, spreading across much of northern Africa...

It covers more than 9.4 million square kilometres, which is almost as big as China and bigger than Brazil. It's easily the largest hot desert in the world, but it is not the biggest overall.

A desert is a region that experiences very little rain — less than 254mm a year. It can be hot or cold. Head south from the Sahara, through Africa, and keep on going and eventually you'll reach the world's biggest desert — the icy continent of Antarctica, which covers more than 13.8 million square kilometres.

ERROR 2 — MOUNT EVEREST IS THE HIGHEST POINT ON EARTH

Everest rises to a majestic 8,848m above sea level. Though impressive, it is not the point on Earth nearest to the sky or the peak furthest away from the centre of the Earth. That honour goes to Mount Chimborazo in Ecuador, and here's why...

Shock news – the Earth isn't round. It's what scientists call an 'oblate spheroid' – a squashed ball shape that bulges around its middle, at the Equator. A person standing at the Equator is 21.36km further away from the centre of the Earth than someone who is standing at the north pole.

Mount Chimborazo is a volcano stretching to 6,310m in height, but because it lies close to the Equator, it is much further from the centre of our planet and therefore closer to space than Mount Everest's peak is.

ERROR 3 — KRAKATOA WAS THE WORLD'S MOST DEADLY VOLCANIC ERUPTION

In 1883, the eruption of Krakatoa, a volcano in Indonesia, was so huge and powerful that it could be heard in parts of Australia – more than 3,500km away. It resulted in the deaths of at least 36,000 people. However, an even more disastrous eruption took place in the same region some 68 years earlier: Mount Tambora blew its top in 1815, sending a cloud of ash and dust more than 40km into the air. Between 60,000 and 90,000 people were killed – many of them indirectly, due to the tidal waves and starvation that followed. The debris was scattered into the atmosphere, creating a year without summer. This led to failed harvests, famine and further deaths worldwide.

CLUELESS ON COUNTRIES

ERROR 1: EVERY COUNTRY PRINTS ITS NAME ON ITS POSTAGE STAMPS

Today, most countries around the world include their names on their postage stamps, but there remains an exception...

The stamps of the UK do not have the country's name on them. When the UK introduced the first postage stamp – the Penny Black – in 1840, no other country had stamps so there was no need to print the country's name. A picture of Queen Victoria was more than enough. In the years since, UK stamps continue to feature a picture of the reigning king or queen, but the name of the United Kingdom is nowhere to be seen.

ERROR 2 — THE OCTOBER REVOLUTION IS CELEBRATED IN RUSSIA IN OCTOBER

In 1917, a revolution began in Russia with an uprising in Petrograd (Saint Petersburg). At the time, Russia used the old-style Julian calendar, which recorded the starting date as 25 October, giving the revolution its name. The following year, the revolutionary government decided to switch to the Gregorian calendar, used by the rest of Europe, which was two weeks further ahead in the year. So in Russia, in 1918, people went to bed on the night of 31 January and woke up the next day – which turned out to be 14 February. One result of this two-week shift forwards in the calendar is that the October Revolution is now celebrated on 7 November each year.

ERROR 3 — YOU HAVE TO BE BORN IN THE U.S.A. TO RUN FOR U.S. PRESIDENT

This common myth isn't quite right, as Senator John McCain proved when he ran for President in 2008 against Barack Obama. McCain was born in the Central American country of Panama, to parents who were both US citizens. To run for US president, you have to be a US citizen, 35 years of age or older, and you have to have been living in the USA for at least 14 years.

CAPITAL LOSSES

ERROR 1 — THE CAPITAL CITY OF AUSTRALIA IS SYDNEY

Many people assume Sydney to be the capital because it is the country's most famous and most visited place. However, that honour goes to a lesser-known city Down Under.

Sydney is the Australian city with the biggest population – about 4.6 million people. But the capital city of the country is Canberra, which is about a tenth of the size and only the eighth largest city in Australia. The site of Canberra was chosen in 1908 for the capital, because it sits right in between the two rival cities of Sydney and Melbourne. A number of other countries' most famous or largest cities are not their official capital either. These include Rio de Janeiro in Brazil, Johannesburg in South Africa and Toronto in Canada.

SYDNEY

MELBOURNE

CANBERRA

⊘ EVERY COUNTRY HAS ONE CAPITAL CITY

It's a capital idea, but not totally true. Some countries have different capitals for different things. For example, the legal capital of the Netherlands is Amsterdam, but the capital city for the country's government is The Hague. South Africa goes one better with separate capitals for its administration (Pretoria), law-making (Cape Town) and law courts (Bloemfontein). Finally, there's the case of the tiny island state of Nauru, which has no official capital at all!

⊘ THE NAME OF THAILAND'S CAPITAL CITY IS BANGKOK

Very few Thai people refer to their own capital city as Bangkok, calling it Krung Thep instead. No one is even totally certain where the name Bangkok comes from, although 'Bang' in the central Thai language means town on a river bank, which may give a clue. But what isn't in doubt is that the city's full ceremonial name was given to it by King Rama I in the 18th century – and it is a right royal mouthful. It's Krung Thep Mahanakhon Amon Rattanakosin Mahinthara Ayuthaya Mahadilok Phop Noppharat Ratchathani Burirom Udomratchaniwet Mahasathan Amon Piman Awatan Sathit Sakkathattiya Witsanukam Prasit. Wow!

NATIONAL IDENTITY CRISIS

ERROR 1 — THE ENGLISH HORN IS A HORN INVENTED IN ENGLAND

Cor anglais does mean 'English horn' in French, but it is not a brass instrument.

It is actually a woodwind instrument that is similar to an oboe, but larger and giving a deeper sound. Nor was it actually invented in England. Music historians believe it was developed in Wroclaw (now in western Poland) in about 1720.

And while we're all orchestral, the French horn was invented in Germany, not France. In fact, the International Horn Society asked everyone to just call it a 'horn' in 1971, but the original name has continued to stick.

ERROR 2 — DENIM WAS INVENTED IN AMERICA

Jeans made of hard-wearing, dyed-blue denim were invented in the USA to clothe gold mine workers during the 1850s. However, the material that inspired the creation of denim probably came from France back in the 17th century. The name 'denim' is believed to come from a type of cotton cloth called *serge de Nimes*, after the French city of Nimes where it was made. Today, more than 400 million pairs of jeans are sold each year in the USA alone. They range from bargain buys right up to Dussault Apparel's jeans, which cost $250,000 (£155,000) a pair!

ERROR 3 CHESS BEGAN IN RUSSIA

Chess is a popular game in Russia. Every world chess champion from 1948 to 2000 except one (Bobby Fischer from the USA) was from Russia or its former nation, the Soviet Union. Today, Russia has more grandmasters (top chess players) than the USA, France and China combined. Debate rages as to where chess began, but most historians think it originated in either India, China or Persia in the Middle East. It had certainly been played for several centuries by the time it reached Russia and Europe, brought over by Asian merchants and traders in either the 9th or 10th centuries.

ERROR 4 SAUERKRAUT WAS FIRST EATEN IN GERMANY

Meaning 'sour cabbage' in German, sauerkraut is finely cut or shredded cabbage, which is pickled or fermented to give it its distinctive sour taste. It became popular in Germany and eastern Europe after the armies of Mongol warlord Genghis Khan took it to Europe more than 800 years ago. Sauerkraut actually has an even longer history, being described by ancient Roman scholars, while cabbage pickled in rice wine was eaten in China about 2,000 years ago.

CULTURE SHOCKS

 THE GREAT WALL OF CHINA IS VISIBLE FROM THE MOON

Despite this fact appearing in school textbooks the world over, it is complete and utter nonsense.

The Great Wall is a magnificent construction, built more than 2,200 years ago to protect China against invaders. Its various parts total more than 7,000km in length. Many wall parts have been restored or still stand today. Yet, even at a near-Earth orbit, less than 200km or so above our planet, the wall is almost impossible to spot without the aid of powerful zoom lenses. And don't forget – the Moon is not 200km, but between 356,400km and 406,700km away, so there's no way on Earth that an astronaut could see the Great Wall from there.

ERROR 2 — GREENLAND IS AS BIG AS SOUTH AMERICA

Nowhere near. Greenland has an area of 2.17 million square kilometres – a hefty size. Yet South America is more than eight times bigger – 17.84 million square kilometres in area. So, why on Earth has this myth persisted?

It all comes down to maps. Map-makers use different projections (viewpoints) to convert a 3-dimensional globe into a flat, 2-dimensional, rectangular map. To achieve a flatter view of the world, some map projections seriously stretch and distort the areas closest to the two poles, making Greenland (close to the North Pole) appear much bigger than it really is.

ERROR 3 — THERE ARE NO CASH MACHINES ON ANTARCTICA

Actually, there is one! It is run by the Wells Fargo bank and found inside Building 155 at the McMurdo Station research base. According to Corrine Morse, one of the people tasked with refilling it, about $50,000 (£30,000) goes out of the machine every week, spent by staff and visitors – mainly at the canteen and station store. A second cash machine is also kept at the station as a back-up. *Ker-ching!*

URBAN MYTHS

(ERROR 1) KILLER ALLIGATORS LIVE IN THE NEW YORK CITY SEWER SYSTEM

Urban myths are tales told and retold, often exaggerated, and explained as if they were experienced by a friend of a friend. Over time, many of these spread like wildfire, sometimes via the Internet, and take hold as fact.

One of the all-time classics is the notion that large groups of huge, fierce alligators have made their home in the tunnels of New York's sewers. This urban myth may have started in the 1930s with the crazy idea that families holidaying in Florida brought baby alligators back with them. As the 'gators grew and became unmanageable, they flushed them down the toilet. Down in the sewers, these plucky reptiles supposedly survived on rats and waste. Apart from the impossibility of flushing a metre-long infant alligator down a standard toilet, conditions in the sewers — with their poisonous waste and icy temperatures during winter — wouldn't suit alligators, as they prefer warmer climes.

ERROR 2 — BILL GATES WROTE 11 RULES FOR SCHOOLCHILDREN

An email, doing the rounds since the year 2000, supposedly contains a speech made by Microsoft boss Bill Gates. This speech contains 11 rules children are not taught at school, including, "Be kind to nerds (computer whizzkids and smart, quiet children) as one day, a nerd might be your boss". Good advice, perhaps, but definitely not written by Bill Gates. The rules may have come from an article written by an education reformer called Charles J Sykes.

ERROR 4 — A TOOTH WILL DISSOLVE IN A GLASS OF FIZZY DRINK OVERNIGHT

Most fizzy soft drinks contain some acids, such as citric acid and phosphoric acid, both of which can dissolve tooth enamel over a long period of time. Studies have shown that a tooth left in a fizzy drink for 14 days can lose a small percentage of its overall weight (between one and eight per cent), but will certainly not dissolve completely in a single night.

ERROR 3 — WALT DISNEY'S BODY WAS FROZEN AFTER HIS DEATH

Legendary cartoon creator Walt Disney died in 1966. Shortly after, rumours surfaced that his body had been frozen and stored under the *Pirates of the Caribbean* ride at the Disneyland theme park in California, USA, so that he could be brought back to life by advanced medical technology in the future. The story, like many Disney films, is pure fiction. Disney's body was cremated (burned) and his ashes placed in a tomb at the Forest Lawn Memorial Park, in California.

NYC

ARTISTIC OVERSIGHTS

ERROR 1 — VAN GOGH NEVER SOLD A PAINTING DURING HIS LIFETIME AND HE CUT OFF HIS EAR

The 19th-century Dutch painter Vincent Van Gogh is now a highly celebrated and famous artist whose works sell for millions.

However, while he was alive, he enjoyed far less success. That is not to say that he didn't make any money from his art. Van Gogh did manage to sell one painting, called *Red Vineyard at Arles*, which is now on display at the Pushkin Museum in Moscow, Russia. Also, Van Gogh did not cut off his entire ear. It was just a small piece of his left earlobe.

ERROR 2 — VAN GOGH'S *SUNFLOWERS* PAINTINGS ARE THE WORLD'S MOST EXPENSIVE WORKS OF ART

In 1987, the art world swooned when a Japanese businessman paid a world record £24.75 million for Van Gogh's painting, *Vase With Fifteen Sunflowers* – that's £1.65 million per sunflower! But more than 25 paintings have since been sold for even larger sums. In 2011, *The Card Players* – a painting by French artist Paul Cézanne – was sold to the Qatar royal family for a fee believed to be close to £160 million. The *Sunflowers* paintings are not even the most expensive of Van Gogh's work. Five other Van Gogh artworks have since been sold for more than £25 million each.

MICHAEL JACKSON WROTE THE SONG BLAME IT ON THE BOOGIE

Yes and no. Michael Jackson did write the hit song, but not the Michael Jackson who sang it with The Jacksons in 1978 and went on to have enormous success with a string of singles and albums. The Michael Jackson who co-wrote the song (with his brother David and also Elmar Krohn) was an English songwriter who released the song as a single, just weeks after The Jacksons did. Both versions made it into the UK top 20 charts!

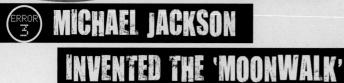

MICHAEL JACKSON INVENTED THE 'MOONWALK'

American pop star Michael Jackson unveiled his reverse-stepping 'moonwalk' move during a performance of the hit song *Billie Jean* at the 1983 Motown television special. It caused a sensation and became one of his signature moves. But American jazz singer Cab Calloway was using a similar move all the way back in the 1930s, when it was called the 'Buzz' or the backslide. American choreographer Jeffrey Daniels performed backslides as a member of disco band Shalamar on television in 1982, and actually helped Michael Jackson to learn the move.

MOVIE MYTHS

ERROR 1

THE GIANT 'HOLLYWOOD' SIGN WAS BUILT TO ADVERTISE THE MOVIE INDUSTRY

In 1923, a giant sign with 15m-high, 9.1m-wide letters – lit up by 4,000 light bulbs – was built on Mount Lee. This hill overlooks the Hollywood district of Los Angeles, which is now world-famous as the centre of the American movie industry.

When it was erected, the sign was four letters longer and advertised a local housing development called 'Hollywoodland'. It was only designed to stay up for 18 months. Over time, the sign fell into disrepair and, in 1949, the letters spelling 'land' were removed. In the late 1970s, funds were raised by a group of celebrities, each paying $27,700 (about £17,300 in today's money) to sponsor a letter in a new, rebuilt sign that spelled out 'Hollywood'. This is why we now associate the sign with famous people and the film industry.

ACADEMY AWARD 'OSCAR' STATUES WERE ORIGINALLY MADE OF SOLID GOLD

ERROR 2

The Academy of Motion Picture Arts and Sciences first held an awards ceremony in 1929, handing out distinctive gold-coloured statues to leading actors, directors and movies. The statues have become known as 'Oscars'. Each stands 34cm tall and weighs 3.85kg, but none has ever been made of solid gold.

The first Oscars were made of bronze, plated with a very thin layer of gold. During World War II, the Oscars were made of plaster and *painted* gold to save metal. Today's Oscars are made of britannium – a metal consisting of tin (mainly), copper and antimony – and plated in nickel, silver and gold. The amount of gold used in plating the Oscar is a fiercely kept secret, but it cannot be very much. After all, each Oscar costs less than £350 to make in total (the price of about 11 grams of gold in 2012). But an Oscar is worth much more to an actor's or director's career, or to help promote a film.

WALT DISNEY DREW MICKEY MOUSE

ERROR 3

Walt Disney was desperate for a new cartoon character to replace his earlier character, Oswald the Lucky Rabbit, which was owned by Universal Studios. Disney's chief animator Ub Iwerks drew animated frogs, cows, cats and horses, before coming up with a mouse design drawn using circles for the body, head and ears. This simple design made it easy to animate. Walt Disney dubbed the new creation 'Mortimer Mouse', until his wife Lillian suggested 'Mickey'.

Ub Iwerks drew Mickey throughout the first short cartoons from 1928: *Plane Crazy*, *Steamboat Willie* and *Gallopin' Gaucho*. He refined the design and added white gloves to Mickey's hands, in 1929, for the cartoon *The Opry House*. Appearing in more than 130 cartoons, Mickey has received a few more changes over the years, but overall the character has stayed faithful to Iwerks's designs. For his part, Walt Disney provided Mickey's distinctive high-pitched voice until 1947.

REWRITE THE RULE BOOK

(ERROR 1) REFEREES HAVE ALWAYS SENT FOOTBALL PLAYERS OFF BY SHOWING A RED CARD

A red card brandished by the referee means an early end to the game for a footballer, but the card itself was a late arrival. It was first used almost 80 years after referees were introduced.

Before 1970, referees simply gave spoken orders to send players off, but language difficulties during international games sometimes led to confusion.

Top referee Ken Aston was thinking about this in 1966 when he pulled his car up at some traffic lights in London. The lights provided him with the inspirational idea of a system of cards for football. Yellow cards would be shown as a warning, while red cards would mean a sending-off. FIFA (the organization that runs world football) agreed to his suggestion, and coloured cards were used for the first time at the 1970 World Cup.

THE LENGTH OF A MARATHON RACE HAS ALWAYS BEEN 42.195KM

The first marathon took place at the 1896 Olympics in Greece. It covered a distance of approximately 40km and was held to commemorate the legend of an ancient Greek messenger. He was said to have run this distance from a battlefield at Marathon to either Athens or Sparta (depending on which version of events you read) to announce a Greek victory. At the 1900 Olympics the distance was 40.26km, while at the London 1908 Games it was extended to 42.195km – from inside the grounds of Windsor Castle to White City Stadium. Further marathons were held with distances varying between 40km and 42.75km, but in 1921 the International Amateur Athletic Federation (IAAF) standardized the distance at 42.195km.

THE 'TIGER LINE' IS NAMED AFTER TIGER WOODS

In golf, the 'tiger line' is used when you aim your ball in an attacking way, taking the riskiest but most direct path to the hole. As a successful professional golfer, American Tiger Woods may often take the tiger line with his shots, but he didn't invent the term or have it named after him. Tiger Woods was born in 1975, while the term was first found in a 1959 novel by Ian Fleming, called *Goldfinger*. The phrase is used to describe a golf game between superspy James Bond and his arch enemy Auric Goldfinger.

SCORES TO SETTLE

ERROR 1
MIA HAMM IS THE MOST CAPPED SOCCER PLAYER OF ALL TIME

Mariel Margaret 'Mia' Hamm became the most celebrated player in women's soccer, featuring a soccer-tastic 275 times (called caps) for the USA's women's football team.

Mia also scored a record 158 goals for the national team and won Olympic gold medals and FIFA World Cups. But despite all her achievements, she was not the player to make the most appearances. Her fellow teammate Kristine Lilly played even more times, with a record-breaking 352 caps.

ERROR 3 MICHAEL JORDAN SCORED MORE POINTS IN THE N.B.A. THAN ANY OTHER PLAYER

The most famous basketball player of all time is Michael Jordan. He was a genius on the boards, known for his great defensive play and his outrageous aerial skills. A six-times National Basketball Association (NBA) champion and twice an Olympic gold medallist, MJ ended his professional basketball career with a huge haul of 32,292 points scored in the NBA. But Utah Jazz legend Karl 'The Mailman' Malone and Milwaukee Bucks and LA Lakers star Kareem Abdul-Jabbar have both scored more points than Jordan. Malone has 36,928 points to his name, while Abdul-Jabbar has a whopping 38,387.

ERROR 2 MUHAMMAD ALI WON AN OLYMPIC HEAVYWEIGHT BOXING GOLD MEDAL

The legendary American professional boxer Muhammad Ali, originally known as Cassius Clay, did attend the 1960 Olympics where he won an Olympic gold medal in boxing. However, his success came in the light-heavyweight division, which was the weight class immediately below heavyweight. The heavyweight boxing gold went to Italy's Francesco De Piccoli.

WHEN HE MISSED HIS OPPONENT WITH A KICK, THEN FELL AND HIT HIS HEAD ON THE RING FLOOR. OUCH!

WALT DISNEY BANNED HIS STAFF FROM GROWING MOUSTACHES FOR A PERIOD OF 40 YEARS, STARTING IN 1957, DESPITE THE FACT HE HAD A MOUSTACHE HIMSELF.

IN SINGAPORE, IT IS ILLEGAL TO GO TO THE TOILET AND NOT FLUSH THE LOO. THE SALE OF CHEWING GUM IS ALSO FORBIDDEN THERE.

FAMOUS COMIC ACTOR CHARLIE CHAPLIN WAS ONE OF THE CINEMA'S FIRST MAJOR STARS, RECOGNISABLE ON SCREEN WITH HIS CANE AND MOUSTACHE. HE ONCE TOOK PART IN A CHARLIE CHAPLIN LOOK-ALIKE CONTEST IN SAN FRANCISCO... AND LOST.

THE WORLD RECORD SCORE FOR A NATIONAL LEAGUE SOCCER MATCH IS 149-0. THE GAME OCCURRED IN 2002 IN MADAGASCAR WHEN STADE OLYMPIQUE DE L'EMYRNE SCORED OWN GOAL AFTER OWN GOAL IN PROTEST AT A REFEREEING DECISION. THEIR LUCKY OPPONENTS WERE MADAGASCAN CHAMPIONS, AS ADEMA.

AULD LANG SYNE IS A POEM BY ROBERT BURNS, WHICH IS SUNG TO A TRADITIONAL SCOTTISH TUNE BY MANY ENGLISH-SPEAKING PEOPLE ON NEW YEAR'S EVE. UNTIL 1972, THIS SAME TUNE WAS USED FOR THE NATIONAL ANTHEM OF THE MALDIVES.

FAMOUS HEAVYWEIGHT BOXER GEORGE FOREMAN NAMED ALL HIS FIVE SONS GEORGE. HE ALSO HAS A DAUGHTER CALLED GEORGETTA!

AT THE 1936 WINTER OLYMPICS, CANADIAN SKIER DIANA GORDON-LENNOX SKIED THE TREACHEROUS DOWNHILL COURSE USING JUST ONE SKI POLE, AS HER OTHER ARM WAS BROKEN AND IN A PLASTER CAST. SHE FINISHED IN 29TH PLACE. WELL DONE, DIANA!

PRINCESS ANNE OF THE UK WAS THE ONLY COMPETITOR AT THE 1972 OLYMPIC GAMES WHO DID NOT HAVE TO TAKE A TEST TO PROVE SHE WAS A MAN OR WOMAN.

RIDICULOUS! BUT TRUE...

GO, SEEK THE TRUTH!

Got a taste for the truth? Good on you! Here are some high-quality sources and resources, packed with cast iron facts, so that you can research and learn more about the key subjects featured in this book.

TRUTH TREK

CHAPTER 1: BODY BLOOPERS

SURF!

www.zygotebody.com
Check out the human body in glorious 3D using the Google Body Browser. This Internet application allows you to rotate a man or a woman, zoom in and view skeletons, muscles or internal organs.

www.microbiologyonline.org.uk/about-microbiology
Learn how microorganisms both harm and help the human body in this fun and informative website of the Society for General Microbiology.

www.bhf.org.uk/heart-health/how-your-heart-works.aspx
See how a healthy heart works and the different forms of heart diseases at the British Heart Foundation's education web pages.

READ!

Everything You Need to Know about the Human Body – by Patricia Macnair (Kingfisher, 2011)
An in-depth guide to the human body.

Plagues, Pox and Pestilence – by Richard Platt (Kingfisher, 2011)
Trace the history of diseases and their impact from the viewpoint of the microbes that cause or transmit them.

VISIT!

Become a disease detective as you explore the history of medicine and fighting infections at the Thackray Museum in Leeds.
Thackray Museum, Beckett Street, Leeds LS9 7LN, UK
www.thackraymuseum.org

Wonder at the brutal, bloody history of surgery and how surgical procedures have advanced. Try your steady hand at performing keyhole surgery on a demonstrator machine.
Royal College of Surgeons of Edinburgh, Nicolson Street, Edinburgh EH8 9DW, UK
www.museum.rcsed.ac.uk

A selection of other UK medical and human body museums can be found at:
www.medicalcareers.nhs.uk/considering_medicine/medical_museums_in_the_uk.aspx

CHAPTER 2: ANIMAL ERRORS

SURF!

http://animal.discovery.com/guides/endangered/endangered.html
Find out information on more than 250 different threatened species.

www.nationalgeographic.com
The official website of the National Geographic Society is packed full of information about habitats and living things.

www.nhm.ac.uk/nature-online/life/dinosaurs-other-extinct-creatures/dino-directory/index.html
Search for reliable facts and details about more than 300 dinosaurs at the Dino Directory, based at the Natural History Museum, London, UK.

www.goodzoos.com/zoos.htm
A great resource, listing dozens of zoos and wildlife centres you can visit, searchable by country.

READ!

Collins Bird Guide (2nd Edition) – by Lars Svensson et al (Collins, 2010)
Detailed guide to bird species from around the world. Will help you tell your mallard from your macaw.

VISIT!

Gawp at the stunning array of creatures and features at this museum, which includes a cutaway camel and a full-size blue whale.
The Natural History Museum, Cromwell Road, London SW7 5BD, UK
www.nhm.ac.uk

Gaze at the world's largest indoor rainforest and investigate hundreds of different plants growing at this amazing visitor attraction.
The Eden Project, Bodelva, Cornwall PL24 2SG, UK
www.edenproject.com

See some of the world's most endangered species, including rare bats, lowland gorillas and lemurs at the zoological park set up by author and naturalist, Gerald Durrell.
Durrell Wildlife Park, La Profonde Rue, Trinity, JE3 5BP, Jersey
www.durrell.org/Wildlife-park

CHAPTER 3: SCIENCE SLIP-UPS

SURF!

www.nasa.gov/missions/index.html

Get details of space missions from the mission controllers and organizers at the website of the National Aeronautical and Space Administration (NASA).

www.w3.org/People/Berners-Lee

Learn more about the invention of the World Wide Web direct from its originator, computer scientist Tim Berners-Lee.

www.loc.gov/rr/scitech/mysteries/archive.html

Get the answers to science questions, from what causes thunder to why the ocean is blue, at these web pages from the US Library of Congress.

READ!

The Oxford Study Science Dictionary – by Chris Prescott (OUP, 2008)

Never get stuck for a definition of a scientific term again.

www.nasa.gov/connect/ebooks

Download free e-books about aspects of astronomy and spaceflight direct from the National Aeronautical and Space Administration (NASA).

VISIT!

Throw yourself headlong into 50 hands-on experiments and learn about time at this famous museum.

The Science Museum, South Kensington, London, SW7 2DD, UK
www.sciencemuseum.org.uk

Take a look at the only Soyuz spacecraft in western Europe, check out a genuine piece of Moon rock and see the stars in a 360-degree planetarium.

National Space Centre, Exploration Drive, Leicester LE4 5NS, UK
www.spacecentre.co.uk

CHAPTER 4: HISTORIC HOWLERS

SURF!

www.bbc.co.uk/history/ancient

A strong starting point for many early history topics, from the ancient Greeks and Romans to the Celts, Saxons and Vikings.

www.historybuff.com

Read extracts from newspapers of the time of famous historical happenings.

READ!

Mastering Modern World History – by Norman Lowe (Palgrave Macmillan, 2005)

A comprehensive reference book for older readers about 20th-century history.

VISIT!

Miss out the myths and get the real facts at the museum dedicated to *Titanic*, which is located where the giant ship was constructed.

Titanic Belfast, Queen's Road, Titanic Quarter, Belfast, BT3 9DT, N. Ireland
www.titanicbelfast.com/Home.aspx

Get the answers to any burning questions you may have about the Vikings and their lives at this excellent museum and research centre.

Jorvik Viking Centre, Coppergate, York YO1 9WT, UK
www.jorvik-viking-centre.co.uk

Essential for any student of US history, check out the original Declaration of Independence and many other fascinating documents, photographs, maps and artefacts at the US Library of Congress online exhibits web pages.

www.loc.gov/exhibits

CHAPTER 5: WORLD WONDERS AND BLUNDERS

SURF!

www.google.com/earth/index.html

See places for yourself, either from above or close to the ground, with the astonishing Google Earth online application. Get permission to download it onto a personal computer to use all of its amazing features.

https://www.cia.gov/library/publications/the-world-factbook/

Get your country facts right with the CIA World Fact Book. This provides regularly updated data on every country of the world from its size, population and official flag to details of major towns, industries and languages spoken.

http://awardsdatabase.oscars.org/ampas_awards/BasicSearchInput.jsp

Seek out Oscar winners and nominees at the website of the Academy of Motion Picture Arts and Sciences.

READ!

The Kingfisher Geography Encyclopedia – by Clive Gifford (Kingfisher, 2011)

A thorough guide to all the countries of the world, with chapters and charts on physical geography.

Pocket World In Figures – (Economist Books, 2012)

A book published annually by the respected news and business magazine, *The Economist*, which gives lots of detailed facts and figures.

VISIT!

Check out the stunning exhibits on human and physical geography.

National Geographic Museum, 1145 17th Street NW, Washington, D.C., US 20036
http://events.nationalgeographic.com/events/locations/center/museum/

For the last word in football stuff, what better place to head than the home of the FIFA collection of more than 100,000 football items.

National Football Museum, Urbis Building, Cathedral Gardens, Manchester M4 3BG, UK
www.nationalfootballmuseum.com

INDEX

ACKNOWLEDGEMENTS

The Publisher would like to thank the following for permission to reproduce their material. Every care has been taken to trace copyright holders. However, if there have been unintentional omissions or failure to trace copyright holders, we apologise and will, if informed, endeavour to make corrections in any future edition.

Pages 55 Getty Images/Neil Fletcher; 82 NASA; 138 Alamy/Universal Images Group Ltd; and Shutterstock: RTImages; AnatolyM; LVV; gl0ck; Nattika; Andreas Meyer; Kalin Eftimov; CoraMax; Jiang Hongyan; Yeko Photo Studio; Ivaschenko Roman; Drozdowski; Sobrik; Marco Meyer; Andjelka Simic; A.B.G.; hartphotography; ancroft; Linda Bucklin; 1167; tratong; Computer Earth; Guinet; Four Oaks; Graphula; Eric Isselee; Tischenko Irina; Rob Wilson; Mellefrenchy; Leksele; Doremi; Brian A. Jackson; photosync; Alex Staroseltsev; Tony Hunt; radho; kzww; FotograFFF; Lobke Peers; Javier Brosch; Jagodka; Scott Sanders; tezzstock; Gentoo Multimedia Ltd; martan; John Carnemolia; Kletr; Jaroslaw Grudzinski; Texelart; Dale Wagler; KerdaZz; Olivier Le Moal; Digital Genetics; Zlatko Guzmic; CreativeHQ; Patrimonio designs; AptTone; mart; skvoor; Jane0606; Alexander Kalina; David Arts; sellingpix; superdumb; David Spieth; Gouraud Studio; Tyler Olson; HuHu; Anton Balazh; iraladybird; Sergej Khakimullin; Konstantinos Kokkinis; Luminis; Block23; Julia Ivantsova; Michael Stokes; Ewa Studio; Dianna Toney; Naddya; Petraflier; Le Do; Madlen; Kirsty Pargeter; Gualberto Becerra; Norma Comes; Regien Paassen; AKaiser; WitR; Phase4Photography; Joshua Haviv; Senai aksoy; Colin Edward's Photography; Evgeny Karandaev; Sergey Peterman; lilac; Irish 1983; Artis77; Nicholas Piccillo; darmaj; Kokhanchikov; Oliver Hoffmann; Tonis Pan; Andresr; Lige Lauzuma; Ensuper; Ozger Aybike Sarikaya; Ljupco Smokovsky; freesoulproduction; Charlie Hutton; ben bryant; r.martens; Fedor Selivanov; John McLaird; Tatik22; Anna Kucherova; Maria A.; Bruce Rolff; paperbees; Terehov Igor; Sebastian Tomus; nito; Ing; hugolacasse.